SERMONS
FOR SPECIAL DAYS

SERMONS

FOR SPECIAL DAYS

CHARLES M. CROWE

ABINGDON PRESS
NEW YORK • NASHVILLE

SERMONS FOR SPECIAL DAYS

Library of Congress Catalog Card Number: 51-10932

PRINTED AND BOUND AT NASHVILLE,
TENNESSEE, UNITED STATES OF AMERICA

CONTENTS

NEW YEAR'S DAY

The Long Look

For this God is our God for ever and ever.
         —Ps. 48:14

NEVER BEFORE HAS IT BEEN SO IMPORTANT FOR MEN TO maintain cool heads. In the face of current threats against the existence of the race we do well to take stock of our faith in the future. Two major propositions will aid us in meeting the hysteria of our times.

I

By *the long look backward* we can find a tonic for discouragement. A review of history reveals that the wise providence of God seems to save man from his own folly. Our own despairs shrink when we view the despairs of the past. It does us good to visit again the well-known wailing walls of the centuries.

In the days that are now passing over us even fools are arrested to ask the meaning of them. Few of the generation of men have seen more impressive times. Days of endless calamity, disruption, dislocation, confusion worse confounded. The ruin is universal. If there is to be a world at all it must be a new world. That human beings can ever return to the old sorry routine and proceed with any steadfastness and continuance therein is a hope no longer tenable. . . . This is a time to make the dullest man consider whence he came and whither he is bound. It is a veritable new era.

No, that is not from an editorial in today's newspaper. That is Thomas Carlyle speaking in 1850.

Again we read:

It is a gloomy day in history. Not in many years, not in the lifetime of many men now living has there been so grave and deep apprehension. In our country there is . . . universal prostration.

This is from an 1857 editorial in *Harper's Weekly*.

Distinguished voices have joined the chorus during the years. We hear the Duke of Wellington saying in 1851, "I thank God I shall be spared from seeing the consummation of ruin that is gathering about us." We hear Disraeli speaking in 1849, "In industry, commerce, and agriculture there is no hope." Lord Shaftsbury in 1848 declared, "Nothing can save the British Empire from shipwreck." And Lord Grey said in 1819, "Everything is tending to convulsion." Bishop Wilberforce in 1800, "I dare not marry; the future is so dark and unsettled." William Pitt about 1780, "There is scarcely anything around us but ruin and despair." Bishop Butler in 1726, "It is now come to be taken for granted that Christianity is now at length discerned to be fictitious." And then there was Bernard of Cluny in 1150 saying, "The world is very evil, and the times are waxing late."

Men have often spoken the judgment of God on the race. They have been fooled many times. Here is the profound utterance of a great American:

I am very afraid, that, in process of time, *New England* will be the wofullest place in all America; as some other parts of the

world, once famous for religion, are now the dolefullest on earth.
. . . When you see this little academy fallen to the ground—
then know it is a terrible thing, which God is about to bring
upon this land.

This is Increase Mather speaking at Harvard University in
1696.

Again:

Boston has kept the form of religion but has lost much of the
power. Jewels and gay apparel are commonly worn to church
by the female sex. The infants who are brought for baptism are
wrapped in such finery that one would think they had been
brought to church to be initiated into, rather than renounce, the
pomps and vanities of this wicked world.

This is George Whitefield in 1740.

A footnote to the present-day concern over the absence of
religion from our college campuses may be found in the
observation that in 1795 at Yale only two of the entire
student body joined the college church, while most of the
students were openly atheists. Today almost all colleges
have full-time chaplains. Most denominations have campus
leadership.

We should not discount the fact that our present world
has many forbidding aspects and grave problems. Nor does
it solve our difficulties today to know that men have been
bewildered and discouraged before. But a historical perspective that recognizes the long, painful, and uneven jour-
ney of the race does help us attain an attitude of faith,
courage, and hope with which we can better face our day
and generation.

The juvenile delinquency problem is a most serious one.
But it is not new; it is as old as the race. "Talked half the

night about the fast ways of young people these days," wrote Louisa May Alcott in her journal in 1868. And listen to this modern statement: "Young women of today live in a perpetual round of amusement. They go about by day and by night in perfect freedom. Their sole occupation is to walk and drive and amuse themselves with dancing. They read the most improper books and the foam of a poisonous philosophy falls from their lips." This is from an editorial in the *Ladies' Magazine* in 1800. Here is another complaint against modern youth: "Oh, it is horrible to behold how irreverently, how disrespectfully, how saucily and malapertly children at this day carry on to their parents; snapping and checking, curbing and rebuking of them as if they had received a dispensation from God to dishonor and disobey their parents." This is John Bunyan speaking about 1660. Here is another: "Our world is full of corruption. Children no longer obey their parents." This is from a statement chiseled in a tablet of stone in Constantinople and written by a prince to a friend 4,800 years ago.

There is no such thing as the good old days. Had the world been foredoomed to godless destruction, it would long since have perished. Whenever we get discouraged about our day and about the future, the best tonic in the world is the reading of history. God must be in it for man to have survived himself.

We have our agricultural problems, but so did our forefathers. Here are the words of a sign on a Blanco, Texas, farm home: "250 miles to nearest post office, 100 miles to wood, 20 miles to water, 6 inches to Hades. God bless our home. Gone to live with the wife's folks." This is from the Mason, Texas, *News*, June 18, 1887.

We have our political problems and like to lay the blame for our ills on That Man in the White House, whoever he may be. We like to predict national disaster because of our political enemies. This is not new. A former president of Yale, Timothy Dwight, apparently took huge delight in denouncing a man who was running for President of the United States. "We may see our wives and daughters the victims of legal prostitution, soberly dishonored, speciously polluted; the outcasts of delicacy and virtue, the loathing of God and man." Who was the object of this denunciation? The immortal Thomas Jefferson, the author of the Declaration of Independence, the patron saint of democracy!

We have our labor problems. So did employees of one of our great department stores eighty-five years ago. They were required to work fourteen hours a day, were allowed one evening a week in which they had to go to prayer meeting, and were warned that "the habit of smoking Spanish cigars, being shaved at the barber's, and going to dances and other places of amusement" would give their employer reason to be suspicious of their integrity and honesty. If the laboring man today thinks he is abused, let him consider the day, not too long since, when the eight-hour day was undreamed of and when wages were but a fraction of today's levels. Only a few years ago working conditions generally were abominable, and children were freely exploited for profit.

We hear much of national disunity. We do have our sectional prejudices, but so did the fathers of our country. Here are the words of Congressman Josiah Quincy in 1819 when Alabama was being admitted to statehood:

11

You have no authority to throw the rights and property of this people into the "hotchpotch" with the wild men on the Missouri, nor the mixed, tho' more responsible race of Anglo-Hispan-Gallo-Americans who bask on the sands in the mouth of the Mississippi. . . . Do you suppose the people of the Northern and Atlantic states will, or ought to, look with patience and see Representatives and Senators from the Red River and the Missouri pouring themselves upon this and the other floor, managing the concerns of a seaboard 1,500 miles from their residence?

We have grave problems of war. We must remember, however, the days when men lived by fighting, when wars were continuous and unending. It hasn't been very many years since no one dared go about his work without the protection of arms. The idea of world peace and brotherhood has only recently been brought into focus. Never before have so many men and so many groups been so greatly concerned in creating a society of nations. We must not be discouraged if it takes time to banish war from the earth.

We Americans are very impatient. We want perfection in a hurry. We dream up an idea one day and want to force it on the world the next. We fought for our own freedom less than two hundred years ago. The fight for world freedom has just begun. We boast of our scientific civilization, but it dates back a bare hundred years. Look at China, for instance. China has been fighting for freedom for four thousand years. When our ancestors were yet barbarians in Western Europe, Chinese people of the better class were robed in gorgeous silks and eating off fine porcelain. When Abraham was shepherding his flocks on Judean hills, China had a magnificent history reaching back more than two thousand years. They had paper a thousand years before Europe. They had the printing press three hundred

12

years before Gutenberg, the inventor of the printing press in the West, was born. Chinese classics and arts and tapestry dazzled Asia before the brilliant days of the Roman Empire.

We are quite sure the problems of the world today have never before been matched in history. And yet, before we pass judgment too hastily, it is well to look at the record. The problems of the present are no greater than those of the past in proportion to the ability of man to meet them. Professor John Bennett gives an impressive list of some of the evils upon which the civilized world has turned its back through the centuries. These include human sacrifice, the subjection of women, slavery; likewise punishment without trial, dueling to kill, and uncontrolled exploitation of men, women, and children in industry. The most significant thing about this list is that all of these advancements have been made possible directly or indirectly by a growing understanding of the spirit of Jesus Christ. They will be outlawed forever and universally only as the spirit of Jesus Christ prevails.

The perspective of history reveals that God is trying to lead men, in spite of themselves, to an ever greater future.

II

By *the long look forward* we can gain hope and courage. The perspective of faith reveals that this is God's world and that he uses the wrath of man to his own glory. We must be patient, and we must have faith in God. Too many people today are feeling that, having come so far, mankind can go no farther. Our greatest difficulties may still be ahead of us. However, that just means that our greatest achievements are yet to come. The long look backward

reveals that mankind has staggered through some very un-
promising situations in search of a better way. It is likely
to keep on doing so. In spite of our alphabetical bombs the
leaven of the Kingdom of God is still operative in the lives
of men.

It is no wonder our horizons are shortened and our spirits
discouraged. We are shortsighted. Our vision is restricted
by current movements of the stock exchange, by votes of
Congressmen, by the private lives of movie actresses. We
are so deafened by dictators that we can't hear the "still
small voice" of the eternal. We need to take the long look,
to sing again the song of the psalmist when he said, "The
eternal shall be thy God for all ages." When we do that,
we find that God works on a big canvas and takes a long,
long time. It is patience we need, and faith.

Dr. Arthur H. Compton, the atomic scientist, said:

Recently there has been much talk to the effect that our knowledge and power are expanding faster than our moral sense. I do
not believe it. Everything in our present world seems to belie
the statement. Rather, I believe that the Creator of our universe
has, from the beginning, had a plan for shifting moral responsibility onto man's shoulders as fast as he can take it. The mech-
anism of the shift is the increase of knowledge. That is the great
propulsive force that pushes man inevitably to new heights and
new strength. The purpose is not to make man happy, but to
make him great. With the raising of the curtain on the atomic
age we have been called to unprecedented spiritual greatness.[1]

God has not deserted his people. God is ready to lead
us onward and upward if we will go. Out of this chaos a
better day shall come. There are always new life forces

[1] Samuel Shoemaker, *Revive Thy Church Beginning with Me.*
Used by permission Harper & Bros., publisher.

at work which God creates and of which God alone knows. When things seem darkest, the light comes. The year 1810 was said by many despairing writers of the time to be the twilight of the race. It was midway between the battles of Trafalgar and Waterloo, and freely given were the predictions that civilization's hour of doom had come. And yet even at that dark hour there was a lad by the name of Abraham Lincoln playing before the doorway of his mother's cabin in the Kentucky mountains; Alfred Tennyson, the poet-prophet of the English race, was just beginning to dream his dreams; and Oliver Wendell Holmes was a babe in his mother's arms. In mankind's darkest hours God has matched the evil of men with an emergence of new life and power.

It is so today. Creative and constructive influences cannot be eliminated from a universe like ours because it is God's universe. We need the long look. It has the power to assure us that our fondest dreams of the reign of God may yet become a reality. It qualifies us as children of the ages for citizenship in an eternal kingdom.

This world of ours has been in business a long time. Centuries pass. Generations come and go. Civilizations blossom and decay. The course of human history is never smooth or even. And if now we are in a cycle when the mists are before our eyes and men are greedy and morally insensitive, and hate and cruelty and injustice and war stalk the earth, we do well to remember that this is still God's world and that God is still with us. God is still in charge of affairs and still, as always, refuses to suspend his laws to satisfy our impatience. It is because men have violated those laws that our world is so dark.

The long look tends to give us a faith in a God big enough to be worthy of our worship. Creatures of a day, we need to humble ourselves anew before the righteousness, majesty, and power of the everlasting almighty God.

Such a faith gives us courage and confidence. It keeps us from being swept off our feet by the emotions of the day. It enables us to realize that progress, if not inevitable, is at least possible. We are the children of the great God of history, of the eternities, of all mankind; and the time has come to indict discouragement and despair as sins of major proportions.

What is our part in all this? Dr. Lecomte du Noüy said:

[Man] needs enlightenment, encouragement, advice, consolation, and hope. Efficient, disinterested help can only come to him from the wise, inspired human traditions represented by the Christian religion, heir to all the spiritual treasures of mankind and keeper of the eternal flame which the greatest and purest men have passed on to one another, from time immemorial, over the bodies of dying civilizations.

To Christians has been given a priceless privilege. In this age of crises we are the heirs to all the "spiritual treasures of mankind" and the keepers of the "eternal flame." God grant we may be worthy of so great a trust.

Prescription for Power

Thou wilt keep him in perfect peace whose mind is stayed on thee.

—Isa. 26:3

HUCKLEBERRY FINN WAS DISILLUSIONED REGARDING PRAYER. He said:

Miss Watson she took me in the closet and prayed, but nothing come of it. She told me to pray every day, and whatever I asked for I would get it. But it warn't so. I tried it. Once I got a fishline, but no hooks. It warn't any good to me without hooks. I tried for the hooks three or four times, but somehow I couldn't make it work. By and by, one day, I asked Miss Watson to try for me, but she said I was a fool. She never told me why, and I couldn't make it out no way.

I set down one time back in the woods, and had a long think about it. I says to myself, if a body can get anything they pray for, why don't Deacon Winn get back the money he lost on pork? Why can't the widow get back her silver snuffbox that was stole? Why can't Miss Watson fat up? No, says I to myself, there ain't nothing in it.

Too many of us have similar experiences with attempted prayer. The trouble is we think of it as a glorified Aladdin's lamp. Under the pressure of some dire emergency we polish it up. Under the spell of some urgent desire for fishhooks or their like we give it a passing swipe. Nothing happens, and we wonder why.

17

Prayer deserves better treatment than this, for it is at the heart of religion. When rightly understood and used, it can be for us the key by which we may discover the deepest meanings and rewards of life. Prayer may take many forms: praise, penitence, petition, intercession, dedication. Basically, however, prayer is fellowship with God the Creator. This fellowship need not be formal or complicated. It dare not be mechanical or routine. At best it is a simple, intimate, personal, informal comradeship with the heavenly Father. It must be cultivated honestly and continuously and in the spirit of Jesus Christ, remembering always that the will of God is our will in all ways.

I

Prayer is *orientation*. In other words, prayer can change our world by changing us.

David Guy Powers tells of living one time in the former home of Helen Keller in Forest Hills. He said he had often climbed up the flight of stairs leading to the topmost room, following the trail of tacks in the wall which guided Miss Keller there. This room overlooked a vast lagoon which later was to be the site of the United Nations. The thing that amazed Powers was that there were so many windows in the room—eight of them on three sides. From them one might see the height and vastness of the heavens. Said Powers, "Yet it had always been dark to her. Small strings had guided her lonely steps to this height, but when there she had only the darkness to greet her. And I thought of the light which must have been in her heart that even in darkness she should love to live with light."

18

It must have been in times of quiet meditation before the majesty and wonder of the universe that Helen Keller made her peace with her world. This unseen world changed her own world. It was a discovery which made it possible for her to say: "I knew then my mind could be a positive instrument of happiness, bridging the dark, silent void with concepts of a vibrant, light-flooded happiness. I learned that it is possible for us to create light and sound and order within us, no matter what calamity may befall us in the outer world."

Prayer can do that for us. It can, from some upper room of our own, give us the larger view of life, of creation, of history. It can give us a point of vantage from which to view the outreaches of space and time. It can give us the outlook of the Eternal Mind. It can relate us to all that has been, is, and will be. When this happens, something happens to us as to Helen Keller. Our vision and goals are enlarged. We discover that the only significant values are spiritual and eternal. We discover that as we change ourselves our world changes. We discover that we can win victories over our world by winning victories over ourselves. When we relate ourselves to God, we share a spaciousness in which there can be no fear or self-pity. Through this sense of belonging to something bigger than our own world we find our world at our feet.

II

Prayer is *attainment*. Prayer can undergird our aspirations with divine power by holding us at our best. A little while ago a lady by the name of Mrs. Rita Beane, of Oak Park, Illinois, was accidentally locked out of her house in

19

freezing weather. She hammered on the door. Her father-in-law, a radio amateur, was in the house alone. He could not hear her as he had his earphones clamped on, busily talking with another "ham" in Johannesburg, South Africa. Realizing the situation, Mrs. Beane went to a neighbor's house. She phoned another "ham," who contacted Station ZS6KD in Johannesburg. They in turn notified her father-in-law that she wanted to get back inside!

In spite of the materialists and cynics who see no point in calling in any God, prayer is no more farfetched than this experience of Mrs. Beane. Sometimes the longest way around is the shortest way home. Often by getting on God's side in prayer we get things done that would be impossible even in our own boastful self-sufficiency. The philosopher Kierkegaard put it this way: "The archimedean point outside the world is the little chamber where a true suppliant prays in all sincerity—where he lifts the world off its hinges."

Prayer gets things done. It opens doors that baffle us until we tap those divine powers that can open doors. Prayer puts us literally in tune with the infinite. It helps us work with spiritual laws and forces that control life. It enables us to work for and not against the currents that govern existence. As Phillips Brooks said: "The little child digs his well in the seashore sand, and the great Atlantic, miles deep, miles wide, is stirred all through and through to fill it for him."

God wants us to fulfill our highest possibilities. Hence he has placed at our command the resources of heaven. When we link ourselves with God's power, we can never know defeat. Prayer makes us restless with less than our best. It puts into gear our finest capacities. It calls to our aid the powerful forces of the subconscious. It gives us big ideas. It makes us venturesome. It helps us make our dreams come true. Douglas Mackenzie said:

It is a fact that prayer is answered abundantly and in infinitely varied ways. No people who have practiced prayer faithfully and rightly have any doubt of this. They know that God has come to them in prayer. They know that he has come in outward answer to prayer, thousands and myriads of times in the history especially of Christian prayers. The mathematical probabilities are all against the theory that these answers are mere chance coincidences.

III

Prayer is *foundation*. Prayer will give us security in a changing world by anchoring our lives to eternal supports. George Buttrick has called our attention to Willa Cather's book *Death Comes for the Archbishop,* in which she tells how the Acoma Indians in Colorado chose to live on the mesa. The rock gave safety. It seems that on the plains the Apaches and the Navahos were dangerous enemies of the Acomas. Hence they repaired to the great mesa, accessible only by a narrow rock stair which could be easily defended. They carried soil to the mesa, and it flowered and bore fruit. They were safe in their stronghold. Says the author: "These Indians, born in fear and dying by violence for generations, had at last taken this leap away from the earth, and on that rock had found the hope of all suffering and tormented creatures—safety." Buttrick comments: "The sand was forever blown in new eddies, the clouds forever drifted, but *the rock stood*. Earth and sky were in ceaseless change, but the mesa was fixed in the midst of fleeting time."

21

All men share with the Acomas the yearning for something permanent, something enduring, something that shall stand firm and unyielding amid the angry changes of time. Prayer is for men as a mesa lifting them beyond reach of threatening enemies. It establishes a homeland for the soul which nothing can destroy. It makes man unafraid of the restless uncertainties of life. He may be confused in his thinking and bruised by tragedy, yet the world cannot touch him. For in prayer the man of faith dares to stake out for himself a spiritual refuge, strong, secure, abiding. He does this not as a self-deluding, psychological exercise. He does it by discovering through prayer the reality of God and God's truth.

To the doubter who questions the use of prayer in the discovery of God one can only say with Sherwood Eddy: "We can prove the reality of prayer only by praying. No philosophy can prove or disprove it. No philosophy or science has ever shown that God cannot put a thought in the mind of man." When fretful men lift their minds to God in search of assurance, they find a divine permanence and support beneath the shifting scene.

> Rock of Ages, cleft for me,
> Let me hide myself in Thee.

This is no mere rationalization or escape. It is one of the highest exercises of the human spirit. It has been tested over and over again in the lives of men.

IV

Prayer is *completion*. Prayer will bring us serenity and poise by surrounding us with the cleansing and healing love of God. After the first eight of his more than forty years in India, E. Stanley Jones suffered a severe nervous break-down. He went to the hills for several months' rest. Then he went back to work. In a short time he had to give up his work again for a long rest. He said that he was shocked to find that he was mentally, physically, and nervously exhausted. He was afraid he would be a physical wreck for the rest of his life. It was his darkest hour.

While in prayer one night in Lucknow a Voice seemed to say, "Are you yourself ready for this work to which I have called you?" I replied: "No, Lord, I am done for. I have reached the end of my resources." The voice replied, "If you will turn that over to me and not worry about it, I will take care of it." I quickly answered, "Lord, I close the bargain right here." A great peace settled into my heart and pervaded me. . . . Life—abundant Life—had taken possession of me. . . . I seemed possessed by Life and Peace and Rest—by Christ himself. . . . The old trouble has never returned. . . . I seemed to have tapped new Life for body, mind, and spirit. Life for me was on a permanently higher level. And I had done nothing but take it! [1]

God is ready to do more for us than we are willing to accept. Prayer is listening for what God has to say to us. Prayer is receiving the healing and forgiveness he offers us. Prayer is accepting the love and power with which he surrounds us. As Harris Franklin Rall put it, prayer is bringing all things to God, leaving all things with God, and in all things trusting God. In a word, we need to let go and let God take over. This kind of prayer relaxes our tensions, calms our nerves, brings peace and quietness to troubled hearts and disordered, distraught lives. It strengthens our tired spirits by filling them with the boundless vitality of

[1] *The Christ of the Indian Road.* Copyright 1925 by E. Stanley Jones.

the indwelling spirit of God. All we need to do is to take it.

The reason prayer means so little to us is that often we are so slipshod in our efforts. We need to experiment with it to make it effective. Here are a few disciplines and techniques:

1. *Take a little while each day alone* to sit or recline in silence and meditation. Let your mind relax and lie idle before the infinite. Beardsley Ruml, head of Macy's in New York, advises his top executives to lock themselves alone for an hour each day and think in silence. In fact they have a silence room for this purpose. From such silences come fresh ideas and release from strain.

2. *Talk to God in your own words,* simply and naturally, several times a day, using otherwise lost moments. If only for a few seconds, close your eyes and invite a sense of his presence. Make it a point to turn your mind to high and holy things just before sleep.

3. *Repeat some definite statements of faith.* Repeat to yourself the Lord's Prayer, the twenty-third psalm, or other verses of scripture. "If God be for us, who can be against us." "Let not your heart be troubled." Or repeat some helpful hymn: "Guide me, O Thou great Jehovah." Such positive statements will redirect your thoughts and refresh your outlook. Some people carry a prayer card with them as a reminder to pray. This gives point and direction to daily prayers.

4. *Bring to mind some pictures of hope, peace, or beauty.* Recall some great painting, like Sallman's head of Christ, some mountain view or some high experience in worship or service. From these mental pictures we get cleansing and peace.

5. *Shift your burden to God.* Pray that you may be given the full use of your powers to do the best you can. Then pray to have confidence enough to leave the rest with God. Many of us say we have faith in God, but we don't trust him. Much of our worry and fretfulness comes from our lack of trust in God.

6. *Pray for others:* your friends, your enemies, your boss, your wife, your employers, your nation, your world. What a wonderful world this would be if everybody was praying for everybody else!

7. *Cultivate an attitude of acceptance.* Don't try to dictate to God. "Not as I will, but as thou wilt" is the prelude to all successful prayer.

8. *Pray not for magic but for things that can be realized.* These would include inner character, new vision, and understanding. Don't scoff at prayer because you get no fish-hooks. Experiment with it until it becomes real, and you will find a simple but profound secret by which the deepest needs of life are met.

Conditions of Brotherhood

Love thy neighbour as thyself.
—Matt. 22:39

LITTLE CARLEY JOSEPHINE LEONARD, GRANDDAUGHTER OF THE late Bishop Adna W. Leonard, had been taken by her father for a visit to New York. The most impressive experience of all was a trip to the Statue of Liberty and the long climb up inside. That night she could not sleep. When her father asked her what the trouble was, she replied, "Daddy, I'm thinking of the big lady with the lamp standing out there all alone. She must get awfully tired. Don't you think somebody ought to help her hold that lamp up?"

Yes, somebody—millions of somebodies—needs to help her hold aloft that lamp of freedom. Who shall these somebodies be? They must be above all men and women of faith. Of faith in God, yes; but also faith in active good will and justice. They must be plain people with an honest faith in each other and with a continued faith in religious freedom.

Let us consider three interlocking phases of this perplexing problem of brotherhood among races and religions about which we hear so much in America.

26

I

Brotherhood is a two-way street and is possible in any real sense only on the bases of mutual sincerity and earned respect.

It is our custom on special occasions to say nice things about the desirability of a fuller understanding and co-operation between Jewish, Catholic, and Protestant groups. We like to declare for religious freedom in America. It's quite the thing to declare against anti-Semitism and anti-Catholicism. To these sentiments I strongly subscribe. Let every man worship as he will. Let every man and every church respect the worship of others and despise no man for his religion, either by open discrimination or by hidden indirection. America is large enough for all faiths, and in their freedom is her historic and present glory. This is fundamental, and everything I shall say is based on it.

Because it is so fundamental, it needs to be pointed out frankly and openly that the burden of interfaith brotherhood rests with the Roman Catholic Church hierarchy and not with the Protestant Church. Protestantism has always stood for religious freedom and separation of church and state. The Roman Catholic Church does not so stand. Father Francis Connell said in his book *Freedom of Worship—The Catholic Position,* published by the Paulist Press and bearing the imprimatur of Cardinal Spellman:

[The Roman Catholics] believe that the Catholic Church is the only organization authorized by God to teach religious truth and to conduct public religious worship. Consequently, they hold any creed which differs from that of the Catholic Church is erroneous and that any religious organization which is separated from the Catholic Church lacks the approval and authorization

27

of God. . . . From this it follows that, as far as God's law is concerned, no one has a real right to accept any religion save the Catholic religion, or to be a member of any church save the Catholic Church, or to practice any form of divine worship save that commanded or sanctioned by the Catholic Church. . . . Such then is the first Catholic principle relevant to religious liberty—that man has not an unqualified right to practice any religion he may choose.

This is only one of many contemporary statements of the aggressive intolerance of the Roman Catholic Church. Such statements render null and void any basis of true Christian brotherhood and put religious liberty in America in jeopardy.

The Roman Catholic Church declares officially that it cannot tolerate or permit any other faith to exist. This means that anti-Protestantism and not anti-Catholicism is the real obstacle to brotherhood. In most interfaith programs it is the Protestant who makes concessions. Is the interest of the Roman Catholic Church in brotherhood to be taken at face value and in good faith? If so, they should begin with a plain statement of their concern for religious liberty and separation of church and state.

We all know many fine Catholic and Jewish people. We are proud to call them our friends and to deal with them. We know that they are not responsible for the official position of their faiths. Individual Catholics and Jews are among our best citizens and contribute much to our American life. So in our common relationships we must judge people on the basis of their character and conduct, and not damn them without cause by labeling them automatically by their faith. There are good and bad Catholics, good and bad Jews, just as there are good and bad Protestants. I would rather trust some Jews and Catholics I know than some Protestants I know.

Real brotherhood therefore recognizes, grows out of, and responds to real worth. Honest, high-minded, honorable, useful men and women win and deserve the respect of their fellows regardless of their faith. Those who claim immunity from criticism solely on the plea of tolerance for their faith do not deserve to enjoy the right of brotherhood, whatever their faith may be. And those who constantly raise the cry of persecution need to work harder at the job of earning the respect of their fellow men.

"Thou shalt love thy neighbour as thyself." (Matt. 19:19.) Who is your neighbor? Was Jesus speaking about gentiles only, or Jews only, or Catholics only? God forgive men for the artificial barriers of religious intolerance they have raised between brother man and brother man. God help men to reach across these official barriers in person-to-person understanding and fellowship shown by acts of friendship, kindness, and good will. Thus shall the victories of brotherhood be won.

II

The right of freedom of religion carries with it responsibilities to the total life of the nation. In our concern for the rights of minorities we must not forget that America was founded on the basis of the rights of majorities, which is part of the meaning of democracy. We do well to remind ourselves that the Communist state and the Nazi state represent the rule of minorities. It is important to know therefore that minorities bear penalties and have responsibilities as well as enjoy rights in a democracy.

When Negro, Catholic, labor, Jewish, atheist, and Communist leaders acknowledge the supremacy of the common welfare over group loyalties, there can be no minority problem. Let the minority individuals and groups emphasize responsibilities instead of rights, and the rights will come as a matter of course. Majorities have rights that cannot be denied by minority objection or action. To block any socially constructive program of democratic action on the ground that it is embarrassing to the minority is to stifle the public welfare. This would reduce that welfare to the lowest common denominator.

If movies and radio programs with a distinctive Christian message are limited for fear of offending the Jews or atheists, then we have a strange concept of democracy.

If the Congress passes or refuses to pass legislation because of the pressure of Roman Catholic of other groups, then the will of the whole people becomes secondary.

If our schools can't recognize the Christian religion as the basis of our national life and culture for fear of embarrassing Jews and atheists, then no school could teach the Constitution of the country. Likewise no President could be sworn in on a Bible. Our coins would have to be reminted and our national anthems rewritten.

If the right of a few thousand men to strike is allowed to endanger the welfare of 150,000,000 citizens, it is an indefensible recognition of minority rights.

If the right of minority religious, racial, or political groups to overthrow or by-pass constitutional government is protected to the point of endangering our freedom, then the privilege of minorities becomes abused to the point of absurdity.

In our desire to be softhearted in such matters as concern minority religious groups we would do well not to be softheaded as well. Too often some of those who noisily plead the cause of minority rights seek to use a popular front to hide a sinister cause. Concern for the rights of majorities is not reactionary or opposed to the best interests of minorities. There is a great deal that needs to be done in combating discrimination and prejudice. However, there is much oversensitivity at this point on the part of minority group leaders. In spite of the cries of the leftists and communists minority rights are protected better in this country than anywhere else. We cherish the hope they always will be.

III

Brotherhood is a positive, not a negative, quality. Most Americans believe in God, in goodness, in peace, in justice, in freedom. Likewise we believe in the human race in its search for order and decency. Therefore we need desperately to face ahead with a united front. Protestant fronts, Catholic fronts, Jewish fronts, are not enough. We need God's front: a unified front of all who believe in American ideals and traditions, in the fatherhood of God and the brotherhood of man, in human liberty and human rights. We have too many atheistic, pagan enemies of human life abroad in the world today for people of faith and truth and love to weaken their energies quarreling among themselves. God is not interested in our ecclesiastical labels. He is concerned with the kind of people we are and the kind of civilization we produce.

God will forgive our faulty theologies but never our unbrotherliness, never our false ecclesiastical pride. God will forgive our mistaken religious ideas, but never man's ugly inhumanity to man operating under the guise of religious faith. God will forgive our queer philosophies, but never our labored efforts to set up fences of creed and sect that separate the family of God's children. A true brotherhood of all who would see the world redeemed from darkness, hate, and despair, be they Catholic, Protestant, or Jewish, is the way of life and survival for us.

How shall men of faith hope to lead nations into a brotherhood that is impossible within the sacred precincts of the churches of God? We who are committed to the redemption of the world need a larger faith for these days. No small faith is adequate to represent the God of all men in the moving and poignant drama of modern life. We need a faith in God that shall expand into a faith in goodness, because so many who say they believe in God are not good at heart. We need a faith in Jesus that shall expand into a faith in love, because so many who say they believe in Jesus are hateful and intolerant. We need a faith in the Bible that shall expand into a faith in the truth, because so many who say they believe in the Bible use it as an instrument of division and superstition. We need a faith in the church that shall expand into a faith in human brotherhood, because so many who belong to the church are prejudiced and unbrotherly. We need a faith in dogma and creed that shall expand into a faith in integrity and justice in human relationships. We need a faith in government that shall expand into a faith in human freedom.

Only some such universal faith can command the loyalties of all thoughtful men in their desire to save the world from the chaos and destruction of war. Only some such outreaching faith can be inclusive enough to be shared by men of many differing religious ideas and backgrounds. Only some such basic faith can challenge the enemies of life abundant that threaten our civilization today. Only some such vital faith can bring into focus the idealism of all men of good will. It can hold aloft for us a shining torch in a darkened time. It will set a star of hope over the forbidding horizons of the unpredictable future.

No one church nor any given brand of religious belief has a monopoly on the two most needed elements of our time. One of them is the restoration of peace and sanity in international relations. The other is the revival of character, common honesty, common honor, common integrity, common justice, and common decency in personal and group relationships. We must all work together if these results are to be realized. The enemies of human life today are no respecters of religious differences. Church leaders who still insist on expending energies in doctrinal controversy play into the hands of those who would weaken our country. They render themselves incompetent to face our fear-ridden and hate-drenched world with a united voice of peace and moral authority.

After a terrible night on Guadalcanal, Barney Ross, famous prize fighter, told of an awful moment in the early morning when he had fired his last shot in defense of his three severely wounded buddies:

We were praying; somehow you learn to pray out there whether you know how or not. And you don't care who hears you either. In a lull in that whistling inferno, I heard all our voices and realized we were all praying. I was praying to the Jewish God. Atkins, my pal with the mangled leg in the nearest foxhole, was praying to the Baptist God. The kid with a hole in his body and the middle finger of his right hand stuck into it to stop the flow of blood was praying to the Catholic God. The guy with his shoulder almost torn off, who was something else, was praying to his God.

Suddenly I realized a strange thing: we were all praying to the same God. We were all using about the same words, asking for the same things—that if the Japs came, death would be quick, that our folks would be all right, and the rest of the company. And it struck me that there was no real difference between us at all; just a little on the surface. And I couldn't help but wonder if people have to come so close as that to death to realize that we are all on the same side and all trying to get to the same place.[1]

We are all in foxholes together these days. It is time we discovered that kind of dynamic spiritual kinship which comes as we pool our spiritual resources against the bitter and implacable foe of atheistic paganism. The God of us all needs the help of us all.

[1] From the Feb., 1945, issue of *The Pulpit*. Used by permission.

On Being a Christian

For to me to live is Christ.
—Phil. 1:21

FROM THE FILES OF THE NEW YORK POLICE DEPARTMENT comes the story about a robbery of a fashionable apartment on Park Avenue. The people were away at the time. Much valuable jewelry was stolen. The detectives could not find any clues at first. Finally they found only one fingerprint. It was on a small alabaster statue of the head of Jesus Christ by Hoffman. The police noticed that it had been turned around and was facing the wall. It was from this one fingerprint that the robber was identified and later caught. They asked him why he had turned the statue to the wall. He said he could not steal with the eyes of Christ looking at him.

Yes, even thieves recognize some peculiar power in the personality of Jesus Christ that makes them uncomfortable in their wrongdoing. So it is with all of us. We cannot ignore Jesus Christ. We are either for him or against him. There is something special about him that reaches down into the center of our hearts and lives. He confronts our consciences and souls with something that is fine and good and altogether wonderful. When we accept him instead of turning him away, we discover what it is to be saved. We then begin to live life at its glorious best.

What does it mean to be a Christian? It is a good question for us on Palm Sunday. On that day the people welcomed Jesus as their leader into the city of Jerusalem with songs and palm branches. Today we may well look into his face and welcome him into our hearts and lives as Saviour and King.

I

To be a Christian means to live *a Christ-centered life*. Within recent years an instrument has been perfected for the blind flying of airplanes. It is said to be the most important invention for flying since the airplane was perfected. Called the Zero Reader, it is built by the Sperry Gyroscope Company. On the instrument board of the plane it appears as a black dial about the size of a half dollar. There are horizontal and vertical silver wires across the face of the dial, crossing in the center. There are no numerals, only the picture of a small airplane on the dial itself. Before the plane leaves the ground, the pilot makes adjustments for the distance to be flown, the direction, and the altitude desired for the flight. From there on, once the plane has started, all that is necessary is to "zero" the instrument. This means that the little picture of the plane on the dial is centered at the intersection of the wires. All the other instruments may be covered up. The cabin windows may be blacked out. All the pilot needs to do is to adjust the Zero Reader occasionally so that the little picture of the plane is centered. If the plane is off course, this will bring it back. There are no calculations to worry the pilot. At the proper time the plane will land at its destination without any other effort than to keep the Zero Reader zeroed: the picture of the little plane centered on the dial. This amazing instrument has been called aviation's "incredible dingus." It is foolproof and never fails. It turns ordinary flyers into master pilots. They don't know how the thing works; it just works.

There is something about this "incredible dingus" that reminds us of the wonder of Jesus for Christian living. As long as we keep Jesus Christ in focus at the center of our lives, we stay on the right course and arrive at the right destination. We don't need to know why it works or how it works in order to know that it does work—gloriously, wonderfully!

Yes, there are questions, plenty of them, about doctrine and about biblical interpretations of the life and teaching of Jesus. There are disillusionments, defeats, doubts. Then it is we need the faith to check our lives with him constantly. We must always bring the rich and appealing personality of Jesus back into the center of our hearts and thoughts. When we do so, we find life becoming balanced and full, clean and complete.

But why bring Jesus into it at all? Why not go it alone? Why not follow our consciences or take the best in all religions? This view is very much like the conversation of two little boys a woman overheard along a lakeshore one summer. One said, "Let's go out in a boat."

"Yeah, and let's go out real deep."

"And let's go out all alone."

"Sure. Let's go out all *alone*. Well—maybe we'd better take God along."

"Yeah, and maybe Grandpa too."

The plain fact is we can't go it alone any more than we could learn to be an artist or a scientist or a musician without a teacher. We need someone along who knows the way, who is acquainted with life and with God. We need a guide, a companion, a friend, a savior. We can't worship, love, or follow an abstract noun or idea such as "The Life Essence" or "The Power Not Ourselves That Makes for Righteousness" or "The Good, the True, and the Beautiful." We need someone we can visualize, someone we can talk to, someone with whom we may have fellowship. We need Jesus Christ as the standard, the ideal pattern, the goal, the divine comrade of life. Nowhere is his superior to be found. To try to go it alone is foolish and futile when the Master of life is here to show us how.

When Robert H. Best began to stand trial in the Federal Court in Boston, he insisted on defending himself. Judge J. W. Ford asked him if he was represented by counsel. He replied, "God is my counsel."

Said the judge, "That's fine counsel, but you'll have to get someone who's admitted to practice in this Federal District in Massachusetts."

In spite of our intellectual pride and independence a vague, abstract idea of God is not enough. We need someone to plead our case in the courts of heaven. Unclean, unworthy, and sinful as we are, Christ saves us. In him we find healing and wholeness, the literal meaning of the word "salvation." In him we find the perfect revelation and understanding of God. In him we find love at its sacrificial best. In him we find life that is life indeed. To be a Christian means to be a companion and follower of Jesus Christ.

II

To be a Christian means to live *a Christ-disciplined life*. It means to bring our attitudes and motives under the law of love.

Do you remember the little freighter called the "Dimbula" in the story by Rudyard Kipling? Her proud skipper said when she was christened, "It takes more than christening to make a ship. She's all here but the parts of her have not learned to work together yet." On her first voyage in the Atlantic she ran into foul weather. During the storm the little ship pitched and chopped and swung and dipped. Her funnels grumbled, her beams croaked, her rivets chattered, and her motors puffed and snorted. After she weathered the gale for fourteen days, all her parts seemed finally to learn to work together, and, says Kipling, the ship had found herself so that if she had been hailed, she might have replied in one unified voice, "I am the 'Dimbula!'"

Some process like that takes place in the business of being a Christian. There is nothing automatic, easy, or magical about it. Being a Christian is not a condition we arrive at all at once. It is a process of growth and development. It involves the hard work of bringing all the conflicting elements of our lives into a harmonious unity under the discipline of the law of love. Just because we are not rotters or murderers does not mean we are Christians. Being a Christian implies that we are committed to the idea and are working at the job of loving instead of hating, of giving instead of getting, of serving instead of being served. It involves the continuous operation of working with our tempers, our fears, our grudges, our desires, our decisions, our friendships, our jobs, our homes, and our objectives in the light of the spirit of Jesus Christ. We literally find ourselves in Christ. "For to me to live is Christ." (Phil. 1:21.)

Jesus is not a weak, soft, spineless, easygoing sissy. He is a vigorous, robust leader, and it takes courage to follow him. "Strait is the gate, and narrow is the way!" "No man can serve two masters!" "If any man will come after me, let him deny himself, and take up his cross, and follow me!" Yes, Jesus calls to the heroic in men. He challenges them to their best. He holds them to their highest.

There is nothing fanatical or peculiar in this. Dr. Henry C. Link, the famous psychologist, said, "No discovery of modern psychology is, in my opinion, so important as its scientific proof of the necessity of self-sacrifice or discipline to self-realization and happiness." Why then should we think it strange to have to work at the job of being a Christian? One of the national tennis champions of America as a lad spent all his spare time for many years in the back yard of a city apartment, serving a tennis ball at a tin-can set on top of a post sixty feet away. He kept on year after year until from any position he could knock that can off the post without missing. Then he entered the tournament and became champion. But not before! Talk about the narrow way!

A. J. Cronin, a writer of best sellers, says that he writes in longhand under the most uncomfortable circumstances he can manage for himself. "I like a cold room, a hard table and chair. If you're too comfortable, it's no good. Writing is a difficult job and cannot be done with the feather-bed idea. I am rather like Carlyle, who said he never wrote or could not write until his feet were frozen." No wonder Cronin cries when his characters suffer. And no wonder he writes great books. Talk about discipline!

So too, if we are to be strong in Christian character and skilled in Christian attitudes, we will find ourselves giving Christ our finest loyalties, our sacrificial efforts, our choicest capacities. Then we will discover life becoming radiant with achievement, meaning, and purpose. We do this not from any outward necessity but from inner desire. We leave less-than-our-best behind when we fall in love with the best. We discipline ourselves because we want something bigger and better! In other words, we try to be Christlike, not because we have to be, but because we want to be! That is the discipline of love.

III

To be a Christian is to live *a Christ-changed life*. Lloyd C. Douglas in *The Robe* tells of young Marcellus, who was converted to Christianity during a stay in Palestine. He came back to his home in Rome and talked with Diana, his sweetheart, who did not approve of this new faith. She listened to his story and expressed relief that it was nothing more serious than that.

What I feared was that it might somehow affect your life— and mine, too. It is a beautiful story. . . . Let it remain so. . . . we don't have to do anything about it; do we? Let us plan to live—each for the other—just as if this hadn't happened." Marcellus was silent for a long time. Then he said, "But it *has* affected my life, darling! I *can't* go on as if it hadn't happened. . . . It is not clear—what I am to do. But I couldn't go back to living as I did—not even if I tried. I *couldn't*."

When one ventures to live a Christ-centered life, something happens that does make a difference. The horizons are pushed back. The mist rises from the hills, and the vision becomes clearer. New values replace old ones. New tastes and ideals develop. Our center of gravity shifts. We become discontented with a vegetable or animal existence. We are unhappy with tawdry living and cheap camouflage. The sneering cynicism of the pseudosophisticate leaves us cold. Life takes on form and shape; we have something big enough to live for to command our own respect. The Christian way is not a set of restrictive rules or a wet blanket to cramp our style. It is an enlarging and expanding experience. It brings release from the imprisonment of sin and selfishness. It takes lives bounded by sex, liquor, and gold, and ushers them into a spacious area of joy and service.

Johann Sebastian Bach was for twenty-seven years music director in a church in Leipzig, Germany. Had he worked only to make a living or a name for himself, we likely never would have heard from him. But Bach loved God and had one great objective. He wanted to use his labors to reflect the spirit of Christ in the lives of the people. Therefore on every one of his compositions he made the same dedication, "To the Glory of God Alone." It was this holy dedication of life that led him in the creation of his glorious music—music that has brought to millions from generation to generation something of the majesty of the Creator and the wonder of life.

"To the Glory of God Alone!" Inscribe that across the portals of business. Write it across the hearthstones of home and above the desk of the teacher. Put it high above the rostrums of legislatures and deep in the chambers of human hearts. Then the petty and baser sections of our lives will fall into rightful place, and we will realize the power and challenge of Christian discipleship.

Yes, Jesus Christ changes lives! He offers us new lives for old. He gives us new faiths for old fears, new goals for old ambitions. He provides new loves for old hates, new hopes for old doubts, new peace for old confusions. He substitutes new judgments for old prejudices, new understanding for old grudges, new humility for old pride.

God help us to welcome him into our hearts this Palm Sunday as our friend and comrade, our Saviour and Lord!

The Problem of Suffering

My grace is sufficient for thee: for my strength is made perfect in weakness.

—II Cor. 12:9

AN ELDERLY WOMAN KEPT REPEATING OVER AND OVER AGAIN that she did not understand how it could be that her husband, a successful, vigorous man, had died many years before. She was resentful that all her family had long since died, that she should be left alone in illness and old age. "Why should this be?" she asked. What had she done to deserve this unhappy fate after having lived a successful, Christian life?

It is an ancient query of course and one that comes to the lips of all men. It is the question of apparently undeserved suffering in many varied forms. The ways of life are strange sometimes and altogether unreasonable. The world is full of people who have suffered heartache and heartbreak without evident cause. Here is a fine young couple whose first child is born a mongoloid. Here is a saintly Christian teacher who is stricken in middle years with a mysterious malady that takes her life prematurely after months of unrelieved pain. Here is a beautiful and devoted young mother whose mind slips away from her, bringing frustration and emptiness to her husband and children. Here are honest, hard-working men who suffer because of the crookedness and ill will of their fellow workers. Here is a generous Christian woman coming to old age in want while a grasping neighbor enjoys the fruits of ill-gotten gains.

Yes, the name is legion of those who know bitterness and defeat through no conscious act or fault of their own. Our minds will go haywire if we try to find intellectual explanations for all the unreasonable, unwanted, uncalled-for accidents, illnesses, and suffering that seem to come unbidden and unsuspected to upset our days. We begin to find the answer only when we admit that there is no answer.

There is much in life that cannot be explained. Neither can it be overlooked. What shall we say of the heartbreak and agony that come from our wrong choices, from illness and carelessness, from old age and from grief? We shrink from the pain and trouble of life, but we cannot escape them. No life, come to maturity, but has been touched with its black mystery. What shall be the Christian's outlook in the dark night of his soul?

The Christian finds his solution not in altering circumstances but in changing attitudes. His victory comes not in running away but in facing with courage and faith what life sends.

I

The Christian finds *peace through perspective.* Among the letters received from a weekly religious broadcast was one that came from an English war bride and widow now living with her late husband's people in this country.

45

Soon after my mother and father died, my eldest brother and his wife were killed by a Christmas buzz bomb. Their daughter was crippled for life. Another brother and his family were buried under the debris of their home for eighteen hours. Then my "skipper" sailed into peaceful waters in October, 1943. No one, unless he had the faith not only in words but in his heart, can know what it means to hear the words, "Regret to inform you . . ." Yes, but God has been good. He opened a door whereby I could use my time and in helping others forget myself. Best of all, he gave me a chance to prove myself in his trust, because now, no matter how lonely I feel or how dark and long the night, I hear that voice, "Lo, I am with you alway even unto the end of the world." Peace is within ourselves if we only cultivate it.

Here is a woman who has found peace through perspective. She learned in hours of crisis to trust God completely and to find in that trust stability and courage. But even more than that she has had the wisdom and faith not to blame God for the bitter experiences that have been her lot in life.

It is at this point that most of us need help. It is relatively easy to say meekly in the face of every blighting experience, "This must be the will of God, and I shall endure it." Or in defiance to say, "If this is the will of God, then I'm through with God." Or petulantly to say, "Why should God do this to me?" But God wants us neither to grovel nor rebel against the events of life.

We must abandon the idea that everything bad that happens is automatically the will of God. Was it God's will that this woman's life be uprooted, her husband and family killed in war? Not at all. It might better be called the will of Hitler. Is it the will of God that a baby be born crippled, or that evil men gain evil ends at the expense of good men, or that cancer cause undeserved, untimely deaths, or that tornadoes wipe out homes and towns, or that slums breed disease, crime, and misery, or that wars despoil the earth? No, a thousand times no! God wills beauty, health, happiness, and goodness for his children and provides for their attainment. But God's laws of the universe and of mind and body operate without favor for good men and bad. Evil exists in the form of disease germs and ignorance. Sin exists as men choose to defy God. Sin and evil often counteract the will of God, and frequently the innocent suffer. This is true simply because we are all parts of the race of men. But God does not create or cause evil. When man is the victim of his own carelessness or sin, or that of others, he dares not lay the responsibility for disaster on God. Too often we are caught in traps of our own making and then try to ease our consciences by saying it's God's fault.

When suffering and defeat come, we need not so much a questioning of the will of God, but rather a realization of his presence and viewpoint. We need not expect God to alter his universe for our private interests, nor should we rebuke God for sending disaster. It is rather for us to discover the love, mercy, and peace of God in the midst of untimely events. For though God may not cause our troubles, he is in the midst of them even as he was in the shadows at Calvary. When we sense his nearness and endeavor to view the strange bewilderments of life from his perspective, we find rest for our troubled hearts. When we associate ourselves with God and his long-term purposes, we are never alone or lost or at odds with ourselves or our world. When we live a surrendered life, we have nothing to lose and everything to gain.

William E. Sangster tells of watching his little puppy chasing pigeons in St. James Park, London. The birds would wait until the dog was upon them; then they would float away out of harm. He was amazed at their calmness and lack of fluster in the face of danger. It was, he said, because they had wings. So, too, the Christian has wings to live beyond and above evil to give him divine perspective.

A man dying of an incurable disease wrote to James Gordon Gilkey:

It's a bit hard to write when I'm lying flat on my back. I expect you know what I'm facing, but I want you to realize I'm not afraid. I've been repeating to myself my two favorite Psalms, the 23rd and the 121st, and my two favorite Bible verses: "God hath not given us the spirit of fear; but of power, and of love, and of a sound mind," and "Underneath are the everlasting arms." It has taken me three tries to write this. Please remember that I'm not one bit afraid.

Yes, Christians have wings!

II

The Christian finds *adjustment through acceptance.* Whether or not God is responsible for our unavoidable disasters, the fact remains we have to deal with them. The changing fortunes of life often compel us to make adjustments regardless of our own desires. Of course we need to change circumstances if we can. However, to struggle against situations that cannot be altered invites misery and encourages defeat in the end. It has been estimated that someone commits suicide every 35 minutes on an average in the United States. Someone goes insane every 120 seconds. These people have not had the deep religious faith and the plain common sense to adjust to the bitter realities of life by accepting them. Many of us are so self-sure and self-willed and self-opinionated we don't like to meet our master. When, therefore, we come up against a situation that is bigger than we are, we crack up before it instead of adjusting to it.

The Christian learns to be the master of emergencies by adapting himself to them without surrendering his moral ideals. As John Milton put it, "It is not miserable to be blind; it is only miserable not to be able to endure blindness." Jesus put it, "Not as I will, but as thou wilt."

We need to get over the idea that submission is a mark of weakness. In reality it is a sign of wisdom. There are times to stand up and fight the troubles of life. There are other times when it is best to give in—temporarily or permanently. Someone asked King George V one time to write an inscription on the flyleaf of a Bible. These were his words: "The secret of finding happiness is not to do what you like to do, but to learn to like what you have to do." You remember the quatrain of James Whitcomb Riley:

> It hain't no use to grumble and complane;
>   It's jest as cheap and easy to rejoice.—
> When God sorts out the weather and sends rain,
>   W'y, rain's my choice.[1]

The famous American physician Edward L. Trudeau spent his entire adult life adjusting to tuberculosis. Of his secret he wrote these words of wisdom: "To cease to rebel, to stop fighting back, to be content with half a loaf when you cannot have a whole one—these are hard lessons, but all

[1] From "Wet-Weather Talk," *Pipes O' Pan at Zekesbury,* published by Bobbs-Merrill Co. Used by permission.

of us must learn them. I have found that the great word is Acquiescence."

We like to have our own way too much. It is not good for us. If all our dreams would come true, all our ships would come in, all our ambitions would be realized, we would miss much of the glory of life. When the load gets heavy, the road rough, and the route uncertain, we need to sit lightly in the saddle of life. We need to learn not to set our hearts on so many things. We must learn to get along without things as well as with them. The human spirit has an amazing capacity for accommodation. And if we allow ourselves to co-operate with life, we have found a profound secret of great living.

It is like the story of Matthew Henry, the great scholar, and the thief who broke into his house and stole his purse. Far from being upset about this matter, the wise old man wrote cheerfully in his diary: "Let me be thankful: first, because I was never robbed before; second, because although he took my purse, he did not take my life; third, because though he took all I possessed, it was not much; and fourth, because it was I who was robbed, not I who robbed."

This technique gives us a strange and wonderful victory over life. Jesus knew it. Paul knew it. "My grace is sufficient for thee: for my strength is made perfect in weakness." Every great Christian knows it. Adjustment through acceptance means not the end of things but the beginning of better things. It relaxes our tensions, gives us a change of pace, brings new viewpoints, and opens our eyes to finer values. Elsie MacCormack put it, "When we stop fighting the inevitable, we release energy which enables us to create a richer life."

III

The Christian finds *restoration through reclamation.*
During World War II a patrol plane was forced down in
the ocean, and its two occupants swam to a near-by coral
reef about two hundred yards long. There was no sign of
vegetation or wood except a rough wooden cross about ten
feet long. It had been fashioned from ship timber and
placed in the sand. The flyers had water enough for two
days. They waited patiently but without hope of rescue.
It looked like the end for them. They could see on the
horizon a tiny green speck which looked like an island, but
they had no way of getting there. Finally one of the boys
suggested that they take the cross and use it as a raft to
try to get to the other island at least twenty miles away.
His companion objected, saying that it was bad luck to use
a cross for that purpose. The other boy, however, said that
he had heard a chaplain one time tell the men that a
little boy had once called the cross a plus sign. He had
said that was what Jesus did. He turned a cross into victory.
"Therefore," the flyer said, "let's make a plus sign out of
this cross and use it to save us." Well, they did so, and
with the cross to support them they swam to the island.
They found food and water and were later picked up by
a rescue plane. It is a parable of life.

In spite of all we can do life lets us down sometimes on
barren islands. There is no apparent hope of rescue except
as we reclaim what little is left and use it for salvation.
Even as barren islands have driftwood on them, so there is
always something left after the disaster and heartbreak. The
man of faith takes what remains and fashions a new and

brighter future. To sit down and mournfully bewail our fate in the midst of ruins is to add despair to defeat. To spend time and energy in vain regret over what has been lost is a sure way to unhappiness. To dwell on our disappointments renders us incapable of new achievements. To live with our sorrows is to be deaf and blind to the music and beauty of life. To focus on our frustrations is to forfeit the power to overcome. Crosses, yes, plenty of them; but by the grace of God we can turn them into plus signs! "My grace is sufficient for thee: for my strength is made perfect in weakness."

God does not deliberately send sorrow and suffering to punish us for our sins or for the specific purpose of teaching us a lesson. That is a savage theology. But God can use them because in them we often find him. Many of us never get far unless we are thrown back on God. Our bitterest disappointments can lead to new happiness; our severe illnesses can yield a rich reward of understanding and personal power; our blinding griefs can reveal values that are priceless. Dedicated suffering can be victorious because through heartbreak and tears we glimpse new horizons of strength and purpose.

It has been said that Jesus achieved God's purposes not in spite of the cross but through it. Exactly so! There are blessings, opportunities, and insights which come to us in suffering that we can get in no other way. Restricted areas can yield abundant beauty. Closed doors can direct us toward things as well as away from things. Small tasks may be done with perfection. Suffering may seem to limit and reduce; it also refines and glorifies. Most of us can gain more from times of difficulty than we can from times of ease. In spite of our stubborn self-will and selfish desires there is more than one possible route for our happiness and well-being. When one route is closed, God offers alternate routes if we have the grace and gumption to take them. God has as many good surprises for us as bad ones. As long as life exists there are new factors and unforseeable elements entering into the course of life by which we may reclaim, restore, and redirect our careers. God does not want us to be permanently defeated. It is when we accept our crosses and use them as plus signs that we find un-dreamed-of victory out of expected disaster. Many of our most creative people and our finest achievements bear witness to this profound truth.

One who knows the reality of which I speak is Mrs. Calvin Coolidge. After a prominent career as wife of the President, she now lives a life of quiet service in a New England village. The untimely death of their son occurred while they were still in the White House. The lines she wrote find a responsive chord in the hearts of all who walk the uncertain ways of life, all who travel the Via Dolorosa.

> You, my son,
> Have shown me God.
> Your kiss upon my cheek
> Has made me feel the gentle touch
> Of Him who leads us on.
> The memory of your smile, when young,
> Reveals His face,
> As mellowing years come on apace.
> And when you went before,
> You left the gates of Heaven ajar
> That I might glimpse,
> Approaching from afar,

The glories of His grace.
Hold, son, my hand,
Guide me along the path
That, coming,
I may stumble not,
Nor roam,
Nor fail to show the way
Which leads us home.[2]

[2] Used by permission of the author.

EASTER

Signpost of Civilization

My words shall not pass away.
—Matt. 24:35

ONE OF THE MOST POIGNANT MODERN DRAMAS OF THE LAST days of Jesus is *The Terrible Meek* by Charles Rann Kennedy. The action at the foot of the cross of Jesus is confined to conversations between Mary the mother, the captain, and others. It is during the night after the death, and the stage is in darkness. When the play ends, Mary at the bottom of her grief is bewailing the death of her son. Then the captain in a strange voice begins to tell her that her son is not dead. To her amazement he makes an unbelievable speech which includes these words:

> I tell you, my good woman, this dead son of yours,
> Disfigured, shamed, spat upon,
> Has built a kingdom this day that shall never die.
> The living glory of him will forever rule it.
> The earth is his and he made it.
> He and his brothers have been molding and making it
> Through all the long ages.
> They are the only ones
> Who ever really can possess it.
> Not the proud, not the idle, not the wealthy,
> Not the vaunted empires of this world. . . . No!

Something has happened here upon this hill today,
Something that will shake all the empires and kingdoms
Of this world into the dust.
The earth is his, the earth is theirs, and they made it!
The meek, the terrible meek,
The fierce, agonizing meek.
Are about to enter into their inheritance! [1]

So it is. Across the centuries Easter has been the signpost of civilization.

I

Easter is *a signpost in human history* pointing toward the triumphant procession of the Christian faith. The first Easter marked forever the Christian idea as a movement and not as a creed, an institution, or a church. True, the Christian gospel finds expression in creeds and through organizations. However, it is not limited, contained, or defined by them. At Easter time the triumphant spirit of Jesus Christ burst all the bonds with which men had tried to control it. It eluded all opposition. It refused to be stopped or localized. It began flowing as a mighty, life-giving stream along the highways of history. Although its leaders were stoned and burned and ostracized, its program challenged by armies and by empires, nothing could stop the steady triumphal procession of the ever-expanding host of those who sang the praises of a risen Christ.

Because of Easter this gospel faith spread quickly to Greece, Macedonia, and Rome. Within two hundred years this Christian movement had found its way into every city of the European world and to all the countryside round

[1] Published by The University of Chicago Press. Used by permission.

about. Men and women of high estate and low came under its spell. It absorbed and used and transcended the philosophies of Plato and the Stoics. It swept forward as the most powerful movement of the human mind and spirit in all history. Two hundred years later this onetime despised and rejected sect was proclaimed the recognized religion of the civilized Western world.

Came then the barbarian hordes, and the might and splendor that had been the Roman Empire crumbled and fell to pieces. Darkness fell across Europe. The culture of mankind was blacked out in the Dark Ages that followed. This was not, however, the end of the Christian movement. Roman legions marched no more, but the disciples of Jesus the Crucified never stopped. The only movement that survived the death of the Roman Empire was the movement led by one who had himself been put to death by the minions of that empire, the living Christ.

During the long night that shrouded the Europe of the Dark Ages this Christian movement persisted in monasteries and in the hearts of men. It kept alive the learning of the past. It fostered the spirit of brotherhood and religion which became the seed of the Renaissance. To be sure, there were many heartbreaking concessions to the superstitions and prejudices of the day. The wonder of it is that it was the only movement to survive at all! During those fearful generations it shed what light and mercy there was in the persons of saints like Francis of Assisi and Bernard of Clairvaux, and in the sanctuary it gave to the persecuted and the poor.

As the Dark Ages passed with the coming of the Renaissance, the Christian Church was ready with new life and led in the upsurge of art and learning. There were Bach and Palestrina, very much in the Christian movement; and Michelangelo and Leonardo da Vinci. There were the great Gothic cathedrals—Cologne, Ely, Canterbury, Durham, York—that gave voice in stone to the faith of men in the risen Christ.

There was the Reformation with its burst of new life and power and freedom. Then came the missionary movement, with Xavier and Livingstone and a host of others who carried the stream of Christian movement to other shores. They planted the cross on all continents, together with education, healing, and eternal hope.

Followed then the industrial revolution, the Wesleyan revival, the rise of the democratic idea with its emphasis on the dignity and worth of the individual. The concept of world co-operation and the brotherhood of man on earth was not far behind. This is the modernization of the Christian movement that received its initial impetus at the first Easter time. It set in motion a force that cannot be stopped. It helped shape the course of history.

Easter comes again upon a world that is troubled and dark with fears. It is no time for despair. We are a part of a great tradition and a glorious company that knows no end. Easter tells us again that Christianity survives its enemies, adapts itself to changing aspects of civilization, and moves on to conquest.

II

Easter is *a signpost of the human mind* pointing to the spiritual and deathless quality of human life.

George Bernard Shaw said one time that the mere extension of earthly living would prove a curse rather than a blessing. He declared that if God lengthened our span of years from threescore and ten to three hundred, then death would be a deliverance rather than a deprivation. Indeed most of us shrink from the idea of life after death in terms of endless eons of a monotonous harp-plucking, cloud-sitting existence. Ralph W. Sockman said one time that he had never lived anywhere so lovely he would like to stay there forever. He felt he had never done anything so interesting he would like to keep on repeating it for a hundred years or a million. Said he, "If immortality means only perpetuation of time sequence, then the prospect would not be very inviting."

Easter is the demonstration of God that life itself is essentially spiritual and timeless. Easter tells us that life is to be interpreted not simply in terms of things but in terms of ideals. Easter speaks of life not only by years but by yearnings also. Easter identifies life not with decay and destruction but with continuance and creation. Easter is God's way of saying that man through Christ shares the life of God now and forever. The real disbeliever in eternal life, then, is not necessarily the philosophical agnostic. Rather he is the materialist, the secularist, the sensualist. The unbeliever believes nothing save what he can feel or see or prove in laboratory or counting house. He devotes his time and talents to the satisfaction of his own physical desires. For him there can be no true eternal life. His reliance for it upon ecclesiastical or theological hocus-pocus is both pathetic and futile.

Easter becomes for us, then, not a matter of intellectual belief in immortality alone. It holds before us the more vital issue of the renewal of the qualities of eternal life in the present life of men. Easter is not merely a formal religious observance of an impossible mystery. Easter speaks a message of crucial importance to our day. It brings the only possible and authentic answer to the question posed by philosopher Will Durant: "The greatest question of our time is not communism versus individualism, not Europe versus America, not even the East versus the West; it is whether men can bear to live without God."

Indeed the political, economic, and moral shambles that is our modern world grows out of a basic denial of the eternal life of God. We see it in the bitter words of Jean Paul Richter, the German philosopher:

There is no God. I have traversed the worlds, I have risen to the suns, I have passed athwart the great waste places of the sky. There is no God. I have descended to the place where the very shadow cast by being dies out and ends. I have gazed into the gulf beyond and cried, "Father, where art Thou?" But no answer came, save the sound of the storm which rages uncontrolled. We are orphans, you and I. Every soul in this vast corpse-trench of the universe is utterly alone.

Over against the answer of Richter is the answer of Jesus Christ, who himself gazed into the gulf beyond and said, "Because I live ye shall live also."

Easter tells us that the universe is not an empty void, a corpse trench for orphans of the storm. It tells us that the world is the residence of a loving Father, from whose care no one may go and in whose house are many spacious rooms. It tells us that man is not a lonely lump of fragmentary matter in a cosmic chaos. It tells us that he is a spiritual personality, a child of God. It challenges man to

60

live by unseen values, ideas, purposes, and goals. It assures him that his dreams and hopes are backed by the eternal God, by whose very nature they are made valid and immortal.

Modern man, caught in the sickening whirlpool of his own failures, desperately needs to hear again the shout of exultation of Shakespeare as he challenged the gloom of the Middle Ages:

This goodly frame, the earth, . . . this most excellent canopy, the air, look you, this brave o'erhanging firmament, this majestical roof fretted with golden fire. . . . What a piece of work is a man! how noble in reason! how infinite in faculty! In form and moving how express and admirable! in action how like an angel! in apprehension how like a god!

Yes, Easter challenges man to a new Renaissance—eternal life now! It calls to us to live like gods! It guarantees, even after our fairest dreams have faded, that truth, love, and faith are eternal. This is the promise of the risen Christ.

III

Easter is *a signpost of hope* on the horizon of the future. It points mankind to the only possible route to peace and universal well-being. Easter finds broken nations black with intrigue and hatred and desolation lying in a frightening pall over vast populations. Easter finds hearts quaking with fear over the "Frankensteins" their minds have created. Easter finds the homes of the plain people of the earth weighted with a burden of anxiety and dread.

What is it that men need most in such a day? Is it food, peace, money, security, freedom? Yes, all of these, but something else too, more important than these. Hope. For more deadly than any material or political lack are futility, despair, cynicism, hopelessness. When we give up, quit, say it can't be done, we are gone. Easter has the only cure for this malady. It lies in the eternal and ever-fresh hope God has set in the human heart, demonstrated by the risen Christ.

This is the hope that saves us from our night of gloom by the light that breaks from the face of God. It is the hope of the triumph of spirit over flesh, of right over might. It is the hope of a better world. It is the hope of a brotherly society where all races have their rightful place in the family of God's children. It is the hope of a world community wherein the talents of men shall be used for creation and construction. It is the hope of the liberation of the common man from all the tyrannies that exploit and enslave.

It is no shallow optimism of which I speak. Granted the scars are deep, the sores are ugly, the dangers are terrifying. Granted the moral fabric of our culture has been torn. Granted the spiritual character of civilization has been mocked and spat upon. Granted that the tender, gentle, loving heart of God has been crucified by the lusts, greed, passions, and sin of men. Something has happened to the soul of man that only God can redeem.

In the otherwise unrelieved darkness of the future there is one great, shining hope. It comes not from Wall Street or the War Department or the State Department, not from the White House or the Kremlin. It comes from the cross and the empty tomb.

For two thousand years they have been woven into the many-colored tapestry of human experiences, a sign of triumph over evil. Against the changing history of the race the cross and empty tomb have been graven eternally in the economy of God's universe as the symbols of spiritual victory and hope.

Why should we bow before pagan philosophies of death and despair? We have the one idea of a father God of love and life and peace and righteousness. Why should we salute any pagan personality? We have the one person, Jesus Christ, the living redeemer. Why should we make halting concessions to pagan programs? We have the only program that will ever succeed, the Kingdom of God!

This Easter hope is no flimsy make-believe. It is rooted in the nature of the universe. The world belongs not to evil but to God. It is rooted in the nature of man. Man is made by God for permanence and purpose. It is rooted in the nature of God. God is good, righteous, everlasting. His truth, love, and goodness survive eternally.

As at the first Easter we must not mistake the big parade for the long procession. In the words of David Barnwell:

The strutting parades of the dictators who promise power, but provide enslavement, . . . will pass, like the parades of Roman legions and the arrogant strut of the Caesars. . . . [But the Christian program moves on.] Undaunted, it has faced Calvary before and knows that the future belongs to that Man who rode into the city where evil waited to do its worst to him, and when all was done, moved on, the Leader of the Victorious Procession that mounts the bastions of time to the City of God.

Therefore this Easter let us again know that the hopes of those who wait upon the Lord are not in vain. His truth and will are imperishable. It is for us, then, to resurrect our faith out of tombs of nonchalant indifference, corroding doubt, paralyzing fear, deadening sin. We must make of it something shining and splendid, worthy of discipleship of a living Lord. God is not dead! God lives! It is for us to quit the ways of grief and desolation, and

> Sing with all the sons of glory,
> Sing the resurrection song!

How to Find Happiness in Marriage·

What therefore God hath joined together, let not man put asunder.

—Mark 10:9

MOVING-PICTURE ENGINEERS ONCE CLASSIFIED THE FOLLOWing as the ten most dramatic sounds in the movies: (1) a baby's first cry, (2) the blast of a siren, (3) the thunder of breakers on rocks, (4) the roar of a forest fire, (5) a foghorn, (6) the slow drip of water, (7) the galloping of a herd of horses, (8) the sound of a distant train whistle, (9) the howling of a dog, and (10) the wedding march. Of all these the experts claim that tests show that one sound causes more emotional response and upheaval than any other. The sound most apt to arouse sadness, envy, regret, sorrow, tears, and joy is the sound of the wedding march.

This is not difficult to understand. No other institution has a more personal and far-reaching effect on our lives than the institution of marriage. Marriage should be holy wedlock instead of "unholy deadlock." To make it so we must discover and magnify the Christian bases for married happiness.

The factor that is most troublesome, that is more disruptive in marriage than any other, and that runs through all others is plain and fancy selfishness. Joseph Fort Newton put it once, "If more people could get a divorce from themselves, they might live happily with someone else." Therefore let us center our thinking around the basic Christian idea of mutuality or togetherness as we take a look at some of the factors of married happiness.

I

Mutual appreciation. William James was one of the most noted philosophers and psychologists in the world. One time after he had written what proved to be an important work on psychology he had a long and serious illness. During that time a friend sent him a potted azalea with a personal note of appreciation. In replying to the gift and the friendly note the great psychologist said that he was reminded that he had made a serious omission in writing his book. "He had discovered to his chagrin that he had omitted from his textbook the deepest quality of human nature—namely, the craving to be appreciated."

Too often in marriage we look for profound psychological principles and major differences in philosophies of life as the chief causes of unhappiness. In actual fact, however, the simple, everyday lack of appreciation lies at the root of much friction in marriage, especially in the early stages.

No one should expect married life to be an endless courtship or honeymoon. But if it is to be happy and harmonious, it must be tended and cared for by continuing expressions of appreciation on both sides. No other things can do so much in melting differences and counteracting defects as simple acts and words of understanding, courtesy, and praise. Nothing is more deadly to married happiness than for mates to take each other for granted. To criticize each other even with good intentions is poor business. Marriage is no reform school. Husbands and wives who continually are pointing out each other's faults in private or public with the hope of perfecting the rough article are heading for trouble. We must always point up each other's good qualities with appreciation and compliments. We must never forget the magic of thoughtful attentions.

In other words, tell hubby he's a great fellow long enough, and he'll believe it! Tell the little woman she's the most wonderful girl in the world, and she will believe you and begin to act like it! Remember we all crave to be appreciated. Let no husband or wife ever forget that if happiness in marriage is to be achieved.

II

Mutual forbearance. Kepler, the famous astronomer, made a failure of his first marriage. On studying the matter over he decided that he should not marry according to emotional feeling, but according to scientific analysis. So he made a list of all the women he considered eligible. Then he wrote down beside their names all the good qualities each possessed on one side and all the bad qualities on the other side. He then chose the lady with the most good qualities and the fewest bad ones. But in spite of all his care Kepler's second marriage was a worse failure than his first. The scientist gave it up as a bad job and declared that the whole problem was beyond solution.

The trouble with Kepler, and with a lot of husbands and

wives, was an unwillingness to put up with the give-and-take that is required in marriage because of the frailty of the two people involved. "For better or for worse" sounds easy at the altar. It becomes in the daily round a matter of putting up with and living with the "for worse." And this takes a lot of patience and understanding, of overlooking and forgiving, on both sides. There will be differences, conflicts, irritations. These blight and destroy, however, only when they are exaggerated and remain unadjusted in the spirit of generous forgiveness and good humor.

Unless there is *mutual* forbearance, there is likely to be tyranny. The story is told of a lady who asked her husband why there was no lodge meeting that night. He said, "It had to be postponed. The Grand, All-Powerful, Invincible, Supreme, Omnipotent Sovereign got beat up by his wife!" No matter how important we are outside the home, we have no right to play the bully within. The tyrant wives or tyrant husbands who require all concessions to be made in their favor, who are dictatorial, arbitrary, intolerant, can make of marriage a hellish experience. God grant us the grace to deal with our differences in the spirit of consideration—to be big enough to forgive and to be forgiven.

III

Mutual fidelity. There needs to be plain speaking at this point. Under the combination of influences of certain schools of psychiatry and progressive education, of Hollywood movies, and of the free use of liquor, the Christian concept of marriage is under heavy attack. Furthermore the cynical confusion in morals reflected in degenerate novels and plays sneers at the Christian ideals of sexual chastity and fidelity.

Far too many moderns succumb to the false philosophy that the repression of sex desire is mid-Victorian and unhealthy. They laugh at the idea that restraint in sex relationships before marriage is desirable. They say that the stigma of adultery is an old-fashioned superstition. They regard love as a grand passion to be indulged with little regard for the conventions of law or moral principle. Such viewpoints are debasing and degrading to human life and character. They are contrary to Christian principles of love and marriage. They undermine character, destroy homes, deny the experience of the race. They bring the heartsickness and moral decay that always come when the sacredness of love is betrayed by lust.

The Christian Church challenges the modern idea that glorifies promiscuity in the guise of liberalism. It challenges our marriage and divorce laws which often allow libertines to make of marriage little more than legalized prostitution. It challenges the education of youth in the facts of life without a corresponding education in the broader facts of responsible living. It challenges the idea that to resist an impulse of nature is harmful and evil.

The Christian religion looks upon the physical nature of life as God-given, beautiful and necessary. But unless its appetites are controlled and directed by the will of man in accordance with the moral laws of God, man becomes bestial and animal, vulgar and vicious. Marriage on the animal level alone does violence to the spiritual nature of human life and is doomed to disaster. Christian marriage is the sacred union of one man and one woman. When either one tampers with that relationship there is heartache ahead.

IV

Mutual responsibility. A preacher was being interviewed on a radio quiz. He was asked by the master of ceremonies which he preferred, officiating at a wedding or conducting a funeral. After a moment's reflection he said, "Funeral. Then I know their troubles are over!"

Yes, unfortunately too often marriage is the beginning of troubles. Some of them are incidental, some serious. The glamour quickly wears off in the white light of work-a-day realities month after month and year after year. Unless there is something more secure holding the marriage together than the fairy-prince, dream-girl, soul-mate idea of perpetual thrills and pleasure, unhappiness is ahead. Unforeseeable problems arise. Personalities change; husband and wife develop unevenly and by different patterns. Jealousy and envy raise their ugly heads. Tensions arise over finances and friendships.

These situations bring rocky, thorny, difficult experiences of adjustment and understanding. We need to know that behind all its thrilling glamour marriage is a sacred, binding contract. It is a mature enterprise voluntarily entered into by two grown people. It can succeed only as it is managed intelligently by a mutual sense of adult responsibility. It is not a matter of sitting around making eyes at each other in a perpetual lark. It involves joining hands, hearts, and heads in a shared objective, that of enriched persons growing in a setting of peace and joy.

To this end responsible persons in marriage refuse to be swayed by vagrant emotions. They fulfill their share of the duties and work. They know better than to live beyond their means. They don't lose their heads in vain arguments. They find in tears and tensions a deepening of the bonds of love. They discover the joy of personal sacrifice for the common good. Responsible married people beware of the entanglements of outsiders, whether in-laws, wolves, or outlaws. They keep their marriage from becoming stale and ingrown by attaching it to outflowing and ongoing ideals, dreams, and purposes.

The trouble with marriage is not the institution of marriage; it is the persons involved. When they act like irresponsible, selfish, spoiled children, happiness in marriage is impossible.

V

Mutual faith. By this I mean faith in each other and faith in God. No marriage can be complete and happy if it is poisoned by suspicion or undermined by a purely secular view of life.

An old Vermont law says that a woman cannot walk down the street on Sunday unless her husband walks twenty paces behind her with a musket on his shoulder. The intent of that law was for protection. However, the spirit of it is often alive today in the constant suspicion of husband or wife that overshadows the other like a cloud. Absolute and complete trust must be earned and deserved, yes, but it must be there if marriage is to be happy.

Roy Burkhart, of Columbus, Ohio, tells in one of his books of noticing at the close of a marriage service he performed an old couple in the back row kissing each other with obvious affection. He made it a point to meet them afterward. He learned that they were celebrating their fifty-second anniversary and were rejoicing in fifty-two years of married joy. Burkhart says he was struck with a remark of the woman which seemed to be a key to their experience. She said looking at her husband, "I trust him and God alike." It is that kind of trust, says the preacher, that keeps marriage Gothic in its beauty, always pointing upward toward the unseen. The two go together. We come to trust each other in perfect serenity when we learn together to trust God.

Marriage is not only a contract; it is a spiritual relationship. When husband and wife share a vital, meaningful religious faith and test their decisions and plans by the teachings of Jesus Christ, their marriage has deep, strong roots. When they incorporate the church into their program of living and engage in prayer or devotions in the home, they discover a divine blending of spirits. They are founding their marriage on sure foundations. That these factors are by far the most important elements of successful marriage has been proved over and over again. It is the overwhelming recorded testimony of the courts, of marriage clinics, and of countless homes. When God is intentionally or unintentionally left out of a marriage contract, something fundamental to human happiness and well-being has been omitted.

VI

Mutual love. A very wise man said one time, "We talk of falling in love as if it were a blind stumbling, like falling into a mud puddle; no, we climb into love." Real love, love that goes far beyond physical infatuation and becomes boundless, sacrificial, holy, is love that we reach out after.

Love worthy of the name is touched with divine beauty and tenderness. It grows and deepens. It is strong and resourceful. It is thoughtful and trustful, pure and complete. When a marriage is based on love like that, it becomes a comradeship of kindred souls that grows and glows with ever-increasing radiance through the years.

> How do I love thee? Let me count the ways.
> I love thee to the depth and breadth and height
> My soul can reach, when feeling out of sight
> For the ends of Being and ideal Grace.
> I love thee to the level of everyday's
> Most quiet need, by sun and candlelight.
> I love thee freely, as men strive for Right;
> I love thee purely, as they turn from Praise.
> I love thee with the passion put to use
> In my old griefs, and with my childhood's faith.
> I love thee with a love I seemed to lose
> With my lost saints,—I love thee with the breath,
> Smiles, tears, of all my life!—and, if God choose,
> I shall but love thee better after death.[1]

[1] Elizabeth Barrett Browning.

MOTHER'S DAY

The Measure of a Home

And thou shalt write them upon the posts of thy house.
—Deut. 6:9

A LONDON MAGAZINE ONE TIME ASKED ITS SUBSCRIBERS TO define a home. Out of the nearly one thousand replies six were selected as the best definitions of a home:

Home—a world of strife shut out, a world of love shut in.

Home—a place where the small are great, and the great are small.

Home—the father's kingdom, the mother's world, and the child's paradise.

Home—the place where we grumble the most and are treated the best.

Home—the center of our affection, round which our heart's best wishes twine.

Home—the place where our stomachs get three square meals a day and our hearts a thousand.

A home is all this, but a great deal more. It is important that newspapers and advertisers center the attention of people on the home. It is very much more important that the church magnify the Christian measure and meaning of home life. For the American home, the guardian of much that we hold dear, is seriously threatened and needs the moral and spiritual undergirding of the Christian gospel. Let us consider, then, some of the elements of a Christian home.

I

The Christian home is *a haven of restoration* for the members of the family. Aunt Fanny, of radio's Breakfast Club fame, told one time about two men who were talking. One man complained that his shoes were too tight. The other asked him why he did not take them off. He replied, "Listen, when I get home tonight, supper won't be ready; and if it is, it won't be fit to eat. It isn't bad enough I've gotta look at my mother-in-law, but I've gotta listen to her too. My daughter married a man I can't stand, and they've got four of the meanest kids that ever walked. My loafin' brother-in-law will be sittin' in the only easy chair in the house, and the only pleasure I have when I get home is taking off these tight shoes!"

We may well pity that poor chap, for his home is not a home. We pity all like him for whom home has come to be little more than an armed camp of unhappy experiences, petty bickering, and crosspatch criticism. Too often our homes become places of endless arguments and controversy, dull monotony and careless indifference to the niceties of life.

Our homes deserve better treatment than that. We owe them our best, not our worst. We owe them not merely our best furniture, but our best manners, best interests, best conversation, and best friendships. Too often we display our worst tempers and attitudes in the home. God knows our souls are often beaten and exhausted with the experiences of life. We need relaxation and recuperation. Homes are to provide these. Homes that specialize in this function are glorious and blessed.

Eleanor Claradge of Cleveland tells about a new maid who from morning until night listened to endless soap operas on the kitchen radio to the distraction of her mistress. When the maid was told to turn the radio off, she immediately gave notice that she was quitting, explaining with dignity, "I do not care to work in a home where there are no cultural influences." Opinions as to cultural influences may differ. In furnishing our homes with modern gadgetry we must not forget the most important cultural influences. These include old-fashioned love and understanding, laughter and loyalty, comradeship and kindness, honesty and patience, prayer and faith. These are the things that restore the tattered spirits of men and women, weary and injured in the work and worry of life. Modern men and women sorely need the healing of spirit and comfort of soul that can be found only in the sacred precincts of a home enriched with sympathy, understanding, and forgiveness. In such homes men and women and children discover the secret of great and serene living. No price is too great to make them so.

II

The Christian home is *an outpost of national security.* In a frequently quoted statement Justice Birdseye of the New York State Supreme Court said in 1857, "The family is the origin of all society and of all government. . . . The whole frame of governments and laws has been said to exist only to protect and support the family." The totalitarian state, however, challenges the importance of the family to society. It seeks to break down the family unit as neither biologically necessary nor politically desirable. Unfortunately we in America are carelessly aiding the Communist program by an evident undermining of family life. Divorces break up almost one out of three marriages. Sex delinquency and juvenile delinquency break up family relationships. The state is assuming more and more the functions of family support, health, and old-age security. No wonder many sociologists are predicting the end of the family system.

This must not be so, for with the degeneration of the family will go the destruction of the democratic state. The wealth and power of this nation do not consist in its farms and forests, factories and fortunes, but in the character of the homes of its people. In all our concern about defenses against the atomic and hydrogen bombs we need to know that the Christian home is the first line of defense. Nowhere can we make a greater contribution to the preservation of human freedom and the defense of human rights than right in our own homes. In the atmosphere of Christian idealism they can be places where moral character is developed, where the rights of others are recognized, and where the authority of love is respected. Homes of free people should encourage the disciplines of co-operative living and foster the qualities of self-reliance and independence. Homes like this are the hope of the nation.

In the words of Grace Noll Crowell:

> So long as there are homes to which men turn
> At the close of day,
> So long as there are homes where children are,

Where women stay—
If love and loyalty and faith be found
Across these sills—
A stricken nation can recover from
Its gravest ills.

So long as there are homes where fires burn
And there is bread;
So long as there are homes where lamps are lit
And prayers are said;
Although people falter through the dark—
And nations grope—
With God himself back of these little homes—
We have sure hope.[1]

III

The Christian home is *a background for personal achievement and service*. Roger Babson said one time, "I have not been able to find a single useful institution which has not been founded by either an intensely religious man or by the son of a praying father or a praying mother. I have made this statement before the Chambers of Commerce of all the largest cities of the country, and have asked them to bring forward a case that is an exception to this rule. Thus far, I have not heard of a single case." More than that, it may be said that the large majority of outstanding men and women who have made significant contributions to society have come out of great Christian home backgrounds.

When Roland Hayes, one of the nation's foremost Negro singers and a great Christian spirit, was a little boy twelve years old, his old ex-slave mother decided that her three children should have an education. There was no chance

[1] From *Light of the Years* by Grace Noll Crowell, copyright 1936 by Harper & Bros. Used by permission.

in Curryville, Georgia, where they lived. So one evening she called them to her in the little cabin and told them stories of educated men. She said they would move to Chattanooga, sixty miles away, and work for an education. They walked the entire way barefoot to save their shoes. After years of toil her boys had an education. Ten years later Roland was studying voice in Boston. He sent for his mother, and she made a home for him there, making the furniture for the two rooms out of the packing cases in which she had shipped her goods. She dedicated herself to his career. Said he, "I learned more about how to enunciate my words from my old Negro mother than from any singing teacher I ever had." In his home today Roland Hayes has a shrine for his mother, an oil portrait by a famous artist. Showing her in simple dress as he had known her, the picture is lighted by a spotlight and has a vase of fresh flowers on either side. Said he, "I have met the great women of the earth, but I have never met one who was inherently finer than my own mother, white or black."

It is in homes like that—plain homes, simple homes, God-fearing homes, homes of faith and prayer—that dreams are kindled, and the qualities of courage, sacrifice, and industry are developed that make men great in character, achievement, and service. Thank God for homes like that today. God save us from homes of selfish snobbishness and help us to make of our homes rich and wholesome backgrounds for lives of useful leadership. For Christian homes dare not be homes of dilettante self-interest, but homes that make a creative contribution to Christian society.

IV

The Christian home is *a laboratory of Christian living*. If there is one supreme function of the Christian home, it is the building of Christian idealism and moral character into the lives of the children and young people. Because of the secularism of our public schools and the scattered opportunities of our church schools, the home must have a large part in fostering the spirit of Christ in the lives of youth, or it will not be done. Too many of our young people are growing up to be modern pagans because mothers are too busy with bridge clubs or their equivalent and fathers are too busy making a living to be bothered with the religious training of their children. We cannot expect our children to have any ethical principle or moral stamina—to say nothing of vision or understanding of the Christian faith or life—when parents are completely indifferent to Christian ideals in the home. Unless Christian influences offset the damaging effects of liquor, of trashy comic books, of cheap radio and television programs, of loose shows and movies, and of parental unconcern, the results are all too apparent. The F.B.I. reports that boys and girls under voting age account for 35 per cent of the robbers, 49 per cent of the burglars, 33 per cent of the thieves, 15 per cent of the murderers, and 61 per cent of the car thieves of the nation. Two million of our young men and women are infected annually with social diseases. Of the one million babies born out of wedlock in recent years sixty thousand of them were born to girls under fourteen years of age. All this is to say nothing of the unhappiness and personality defects of those whose training ignores God.

There have been improvements in working, living, health, and educational conditions in the past fifty years. The fact remains, however, that such environmental factors as tile bathrooms, convertibles, air conditioning, and vitamin pills cannot themselves produce better men and women. There must be a like improvement in moral character and spiritual experience. This is the job of the Christian home. It's not the kind of house but the kind of home that matters. Too many homes are run by children. Parents in our homes need a revival of discipline. They dare not surrender to the children. Parents, however, are not always to blame. Teen-age youths of good homes often violate their home training in a false desire to be smart and popular. They ought to be ashamed of themselves. Young people as well as parents have a responsibility to the home.

There is one answer and only one: to make the spirit of Jesus Christ a functioning and guiding ideal at the center of the home life. We don't need the preacher to tell us that. Every Mother of the Year selected by the Golden Rule Foundation has said the same thing. Divorce court judges and social workers say it. When Mrs. Clara T. Murray was honored for twenty-five years in probation work in Chicago, she gave three simple rules for young people to stay out of trouble. These rules were drawn from working with 108,750 cases. They were: (1) Make your mother your friend and companion. (2) Keep out of taverns and night clubs. (3) Never forget your religious training. Editorial writers are saying it. Even business institutions are saying it. For several years the Institute of Life Insurance has run a full-page ad in 375 newspapers pointing up the need for religion in the home. It shows a picture of a mother hearing the bedtime prayers of her two children. The ad carries the words: "We teach our children our faith so that they will not be alone as they face the world." The sponsors say they have never before had such a tremendous response to any publicity.

We must renew a spirit of deep spiritual dedication to God in our homes if they are to perform their high function. Bishop Francis Warne one time was making an appeal for funds before a native congregation in India. A poor widow wrote on her card: "I will give Christ six annas and my baby boy." The money amounted to twelve cents, and the infant was only one in India's millions. Yet the widow never forgot that her child was dedicated. She raised him in a vital Christian faith in an unchristian land. Now a man, that child is one of the great Christian leaders of India. There was the American father of little means but great faith whose simple will contained this statement: "I desire to bequeath to my children and their families my testimony to the truth and preciousness of the gospel of Jesus Christ. This heritage of the Christian faith is of infinitely more value than any house, land, or barns. I hereby bequeath and devise it to them." And then there is this prayer of a mother after the children had gone to bed: "They are asleep, O God, and I am tired. Make me all I want them to be, strong and true and greathearted. Let me mend their souls as well as attend to their bodies. Help me to learn the secret of trust in thee from their trust in me." From such great dedications come great homes.

STUDENT DAY

One Solitary Life

I am the light of the world.
—John 8:12

ONE OF THE MOST FASCINATING THINGS ABOUT JESUS IS THE simple fact that he was born as a baby and grew up through childhood and youth to manhood—that he lived the life of an individual human being like you and me. God, in his infinite concern for human life and the world, did not appoint a committee or dictate a memorandum. Nor did he set up an organization or call a convention. What he did was to bring a life into the world. One solitary life. It was as if he said to men that one single person can be of significant influence in a world of persons.

In a recent report the Library of Congress revealed that in its immense collection of books, the world's largest, there are far more about Jesus than about any other character in history. The figures are: Jesus Christ, 5,152; Abraham Lincoln, 2,319; George Washington, 1,755; and William Shakespeare, 1,172. All of which confirms the well-known words of James A. Francis:

He never wrote a book. He never held an office. He never owned a home. He never had a family. He never went to college. He never traveled two hundred miles from the place where

83

he was born. He never did any of the things that usually accompany greatness. He had no credentials but himself. . . . [Yet] I am far within the mark when I say that all the armies that ever marched, and all the navies that ever were built, and all the parliaments that ever sat, and all the kings that ever reigned, put together, have not affected the life of man upon this earth as powerfully as has that *one solitary life.*

In a day when society is so complex that a young person is likely to feel buried in the crowd, we need to recapture this idea. It is all too easy to assume that we as individuals do not count in the group. We easily excuse ourselves from personal moral responsibility by hiding behind social custom. We assume it is of no importance what any one person thinks or does. Therefore we don't care what we think or do. We are faced with powerful social forces and feel helpless to challenge them by individual effort.

Let's consider, then, some of the secrets of one solitary life's influence in terms of today. In this way we may discover how a young man or a young woman may make his own solitary life count.

I

Jesus *identified himself with a great idea.* He lived for a supreme objective: the Kingdom of God. "To this end was I born and for this cause came I into the world, that I should bear witness unto the truth." (John 18:37.) Jesus had a main-track mind. He would not be sidetracked. He refused to fritter away his energies. He delivered the full impact of his total life toward one great goal. Here is one secret of how one life can be important even in days like these. The difficulty with us too often is not that we don't give ourselves for something, but that we give ourselves for something too little.

A striking example of this was pointed out not long ago. Back in 1923 eight of the world's most successful financiers met at the Edgewater Beach Hotel in Chicago.

Present were:
The president of the largest independent steel company.
The president of the largest utility company.
The greatest wheat speculator.
The president of the New York Stock Exchange.
A member of the President's Cabinet.
The greatest "bear" in Wall Street.
The president of the Bank for International Settlements.
The head of the world's greatest monopoly.

Collectively these tycoons controlled more wealth than there was in the U.S. Treasury, and for years newspapers and magazines had been printing their success stories and urging the youth of the nation to follow their examples. Twenty-five years later let's see what happened to these men.

The president of the largest independent steel company— Charles Schwab—lived on borrowed money the last five years of his life and died broke.

The greatest wheat speculator—Arthur Cutten—died abroad, insolvent.

The president of the New York Stock Exchange—Richard Whitney—was recently released from Sing Sing.

The member of the President's Cabinet—Albert Fall—was pardoned from prison so he could die at home.

The greatest "bear" in Wall Street—Jesse Livermore—committed suicide.

The president of the Bank for International Settlements—Leon Fraser—committed suicide.

The head of the world's greatest monopoly—Ivar Kreuger— committed suicide.[1]

[1] Billy Rose in the *New York Herald Tribune*, November 8, 1948. Used by permission.

What was the matter with these men? Their lives illus-
trate the danger of selfishness. Most of them gave themselves to no cause greater than their own selfish lust for
power. They had influence, yes, but it was too often a
misdirected and evil influence. It fed on greed, lived on
trickery, fattened on the heartbreak of their fellows. The
influence of one selfish man too often proves a boomerang
and leaves blight and destruction in its wake.

Consider, in contrast, the influence of this one solitary
life which had no earthly trappings but which was identified with a great idea, the idea of the kingdom of God.
Lloyd C. Douglas, the distinguished American novelist,
one time challenged the critics of Jesus Christ to delete
Jesus from our present life. Said he:

Let the critic drop Jesus' name and the allusions to his career
from his own speech. Let him resolve that he will consistently
refuse to enter any building in which there is an inscription of
honor to this teacher; that he will not again look upon any statue
or painting which has to do with this man or his message; that
he will avoid hearing any music which involves this theme; that
he will not read any more history in which the cause of Christianity is at issue. Let him proceed further and discontinue the
use of any benefits, inventions, or energies produced as a direct
result of education fostered by Christianity. . . . He will discover
that long before he has finished deleting Jesus from his life he
has jeopardized everything he holds in esteem.[2]

Here, then, is one way to make a single life truly influen-
tial. It is to serve God instead of gold, to invest yourself
in men instead of markets. It is to live for long-term, instead
of temporary, values. It is to put the church first instead of

[2] From *These Sayings of Mine*, published by Chas. Scribner's Sons.
Used by permission.

last. It is to identify yourself with great causes instead of petty satisfactions. Do this, and one solitary life, however humble, becomes great in stature and matchless in its endless influence among men.

II

Jesus *multiplied himself by the contagion of truth and goodness*. He was not one who lived to himself. Jesus touched other lives constantly and always left them glowing with the warmth and light of his personality. He made friends and friends made disciples. From life to life and heart to heart was carried something of the cleansing, healing, inspiring power of his own faith. If evil multiplies, so do truth, goodness, and love. We must never forget that. One solitary life, glowing with the light of God, never lives to itself or in vain. It is a center of radiating circles of love and hope. This has been the testimony of history. It is just as true today.

Carl Sandburg in one of his books about America, *Remembrance Rock*, tells of young William Bradford, later to become the first governor of the colonists. Bradford was leading the secret meetings in England of those planning to go to the New World in order to find religious freedom. He was a humble man, born in Austerfield and at the age of twelve put to plowing in the fields. The other people were simple people, too. They were drawn to this man by his great earnestness. At one of these little meetings, with his eyes lighted, as Sandburg says, "by a hunger no man can read," Bradford talked to his little band of peasant folk. He said, "Out of small beginnings great things have been produced by God's hand that made all things of nothing and gives being to all things that are—and as one small candle may light a thousand, so the light here kindled may shine to many, yea in some sort to a whole nation." That's it, you see! The pity of it is that too many of William Bradford's descendants sit around and wring their hands about the state of the world. They excuse themselves for doing nothing by saying, "What can I do? That sounds good, but I'm not a William Bradford, and I don't want to found a New World. What can I do to multiply myself?"

Take Basil Robert McAllister, for instance, a small man, a bachelor, a bank clerk in the Bronx. After the war he began to hear from some of his friends in Finland about the very great need there. He did not refer the letters to a committee, or even write a check. He did something much better. He spent every spare minute and every spare penny for packages of food and clothing. He collected what he could from friends and bought the rest himself. He sent 300 pairs of shoes, 480 sets of underwear, dozens of overcoats and blankets, hundreds of cans of food. In two years he sent 600 packages totaling 6,000 pounds. He helped friends of his original friends—many families. Later his Finnish friends asked him to come over and visit. Armed with hundreds of lollipops for the children, McAllister went. The children had been taught to say, "Welcome to Finland, Uncle Bob." Back in America later in his lonely one-room apartment in the Bronx, Bob McAllister told reporters he had spent most of his life savings on his "one-man Marshall Plan" and had spent $700 in one year for postage alone. Said he, "I spent as much as I could spare. Don't you think it's more important for kids to have milk and shoes than to watch the bankroll?" One solitary life multiplying itself by the contagion of goodness! By such means more than by acts of Congress are the ways of peace and international friendship cemented and guaranteed.

It is so, too, with juvenile delinquency. What can one person do? This was what a one-room rural schoolteacher asked herself in 1905 in Clarinda, Iowa. Jessie Shambaugh was her name. The problem was present then, too. She invited some of the larger boys who had been troublesome to stay after school and talk about judging corn. She interested them in improving the corn on their farms, and encouraged a friendly rivalry among them. Interest grew and the idea spread. They entered their corn in the show at Omaha and won. That was the beginning of the 4-H Clubs of America which now have approximately two million members holding to the ideals of Head, Heart, Hands, and Health. This is one of the most wholesome and effective character and citizenship building programs ever developed. It all started with a one-room rural schoolteacher who multiplied herself by the simple contagion of goodness.

Of such is the kingdom of God. Let no man withhold his light because it is dim or be silent because his voice is weak. In the strange ways of God one small candle may light a thousand, and words that speak of the love of Christ shall be heard around the earth. We need organizations, laws, and programs of social action, to be sure. But these are powerless without the combined power of powerful personalities.

III

Jesus *was expendable for his convictions.* This one solitary life would never have exerted the influence it has if

Jesus had been simply a believer in God, and a teacher of love and goodness. It was because he was willing to give of himself for his cause that his personality had the cutting edge it did, and his ministry its continuing power through the years. So it is with our one life. We make it count when we dare invest it for what we believe, even though at a sacrifice. It is the things men do beyond the ordinary and expected that advance the kingdom of God.

Meeting Mrs. Daniel A. Poling one morning after church reminded me of the death of her son. He was one of the four chaplains in World War II who went down with their ship because they gave their life preservers to others even though they were not required to do so. Four ordinary chaplains thus became immortal in their testimony to the power of faith that compels men to be expendable for their convictions.

A young woman, an air-line stewardess, left that glamorous work recently to become a missionary. She said that in caring for prosperous travelers in flights to Puerto Rico, Madrid, Bombay, and Cairo, she saw "streets filled with lepers and beggars, poverty-stricken homes and people who needed help." She was challenged to invest her one solitary life in relieving human suffering. She finds the prospect more absorbing than flying. That's going to be a life of influence.

Then there is the prosperous merchant who has cut out the liquor department in his store. He said he began mentally to follow those bottles home and to realize the trouble they caused. His conscience bothered him. He voluntarily gave up the two-million-dollar-a-year liquor business out of which he was making a clear profit of

$600,000 annually. More merchants and public leaders must be willing to sacrifice for the sake of conscience and decency. Then we will get farther than we would by relying upon social legislation—to which we give lip service unsupported by sincere action. It is when our good intentions become convictions and our convictions drive us to action that one life counts.

The music teacher in a large junior high school in Texas was concerned that the pupils have some religious idealism as a part of their educational program. She did not wait for the state board or the Supreme Court to act. Singlehanded and completely on her own, outside of her regular heavy schedule, she set up a program of daily devotionals. These are sent out over the school's public address system into every classroom throughout the school for five minutes at the beginning of the day. She herself writes many of the messages, pointing up the religious meaning of everyday life. A school pupil reads each message. Some of them are prepared by children and other teachers. Religious music is broadcasted from records. It is a school project; no churches or preachers are involved. Religion in the schools is a difficult problem, yet she has conducted this program as a labor of love until it has become a powerful influence in the life of the school. Other schools have taken it up, and the story has been told in national magazines.

The reason many of us do not make our one solitary life count for more is that we are afraid of being expendable for our convictions. We want to be safe and comfortable. "Let George do it," we say. We are too often like the Basic English translation of Winston Churchill's famous saying: "I have nothing to offer but blood, toil, tears, and sweat."

In Basic English this becomes: "I have nothing to offer but red liquid, work, eyewash, and body water." God pity us if we offer red liquid instead of blood, eyewash instead of tears, and body water instead of sweat on the altars of God and humanity.

In spite of our easy excuses, therefore, one single life is not lost in the shuffle. It is not a hopeless zero in a machine age. It need not be submerged in the mass. One young life, however humble, can exert influences, conscious and unconscious, far beyond itself. It can help build or tear down the Church. It can dignify or degrade a profession. It can bless or curse a home. It can enrich or cheapen a community. It can advance or hinder solutions to social problems. It can be a credit or a disgrace to the kingdom of God. The point is, What are you doing with your one solitary life?

FATHER'S DAY

The Measure of a Man

He shall be like a tree planted by the rivers of water.
—Ps. 1:3

THE MEANING OF FATHER'S DAY IS FOCUSED IN OUR SUBJECT,
"The Measure of a Man." We honor fathers and pray God
that the fathers of our land will live up to their high opportunities and responsibilities. We fathers had better look to
our laurels. In a poll fifteen hundred children around thirteen years old in the Massachusetts schools were asked
what person they wanted to be like ten years from that date.
Only 10 per cent said they wanted to be like dad!

Life is no bowl of cherries for any of us. If we are to
meet its difficult challenge and win, we need all the divine
help and guidance we can get from Christian standards.
What are some of God's measurements of a man's life?

I

God measures men by *the genuineness of their personal
worth*. Dr. Frederick H. Pough, of the American Museum
of Natural History, is one of the foremost authorities on
precious gems. He tells of a method used by dishonest
jewel dealers to change and improve the color of cheap
stones by X-ray treatment and thus increase their value.

When treated with X ray, for instance, white topaz changes to brown-purple, pinkish sapphires turn to brilliant amber, and so on. These changes remain so long as the stones are kept in the dark and at room temperature. The stones revert to their original color when exposed to heat or sunlight. Some stones, like emeralds or opals, show no change under X-ray treatment and thus defy fraud.

Men are like precious stones. They sometimes absorb coloration from exposure to a Christian environment which allows them to pass for more than they are really worth. They sometimes take on a coating of culture and respectability for the sake of some short-term objective. They sometimes change color to suit changing situations. Thus often unintentional hypocrisy remains undetected so long as everything goes well. But when they are tested by some strong temptation, they show their true colors. When faced with a bitter experience or exposure to the white light and heat of truth, they quickly revert to type.

God does not measure men by some surface appearance, but by the way they stand up in unfavorable, as well as favorable, situations. The true quality of a man's life is more in evidence when he is off guard than when he is on guard. The true measure of a man lies in the genuineness of his soul—its capacity to color his environment rather than to take color from it. If he is going to be good, let him be good all the way through. Otherwise he will discover too late that "no man can serve two masters." If he wants to measure up, let him remember that God judges men not by outward acts alone but by inward motives and attitudes. It could be that most of us need to clean the inside of the cup.

II

God measures men by *their willingness to deal honorably with their fellow men.* When men treat others shabbily, they measure themselves as little men. All too many of us fall short of God's measurement because we choose to deal with our fellow men harshly and critically instead of generously and sympathetically. We like to treat others on the basis of prejudice instead of principle. We judge them emotionally instead of objectively. As Arch Jarrell put it:

If you like him, he is a liberal; if you don't, he's a red . . . If you like him, he's a conservative; if you don't, he's a fascist reactionary . . . If you like him, he's discriminating in his friendships; if you don't, he's a snob . . . If you like him, he's a gay dog; if you don't, he's an old goat.

The true measure of a man is not how he treats those who happen to agree with him, but how he deals with those who disagree with him. God has made us all different. Each of us is an individual in his own right. Every man is entitled to our respect and understanding as a child of God. Let a man deal fairly and honestly with all men. Let him steadfastly refuse to cheat, or lie, or take unfair advantage of his fellow man. Such a man rates with God.

George Gallup tells of a professor of physics who drew a chalk line on the blackboard. He then asked the members of the class to guess the length of the line. It happened to be five feet. There were many varied guesses. Some guessed seven feet, some four, some eight, and some only three. But the interesting point of the experiment was that the average of all their guesses was exactly correct—five feet. No one is perfect in his judgments, but the sum of all

honest judgments is surprisingly right. This is the basis of
the Christian idea of the dignity and worth of personality.
It is the foundation of democratic society. When a man in-
sists that he alone is right and everyone else is wrong, he
becomes a petty dictator. When men refuse to play the
game unless it is played their way, when they pick up their
marbles and go home, they only betray their littleness. To
live successfully in a society of differing individuals it is
essential that men co-operate on the basis of mutual respect
and understanding. This can be done only as men deal
honestly and in good faith with each other. God respects
our personal opinions. He also measures us by our willingness to give and take in discovering a common basis of life.
This is true in business, in the home, in the nation, and in
the church.

III

God measures men by *their moral character* rather than
by their intellectual or financial attainment. Sydney J.
Harris wrote in one of his columns in the Chicago *Daily
News* about a young college graduate who had come to
him for advice on his career. Harris said he was sorry the
chap bragged on his intelligence as though that were the
most important virtue.

He will learn how wrong he is in the years to come. Intelligence is often as much a handicap as an asset; the brightest people find it hardest to get along with others. Nobody likes a
thinking machine. Besides, character is a good deal more important than intellect. The most intelligent people are not the
best people, and are very liable to be the worst. Our educational
system has failed because it tries to train the intellect without
at the same time trying to strengthen the moral sense. It has

aimed at turning out better lawyers, better mechanics, better salesmen. But what we need most today are better men. Only the moral virtues can bring the good life to all people.[1]

If men are to measure up to the tough demands of modern life, they must be morally alive as well as intellectually alert. Our whole economic and social structure, as well as human personality, is bound together and exists in any permanent and decent form only as it is rooted on moral principle. When men lie, murder, cheat, steal, lust, without remorse or conscience, it's high time even educated men learned that the moral laws of God have not been repealed. And all the psychiatrists, cynics, and intellectuals can't excuse sinful men from suffering the consequences of their own acts.

Education of the mind without an education of the moral sense is dangerous to life and society. When Einstein wrote his famous transformation equation, he was not thinking of its military application. Out of that equation, however, came one of the principles on which the atomic bomb was based. The great two-hundred-inch telescope on Mount Palomar will expand our comprehension of the distant limits of space and time. The same instrument, seeking the secrets of astrophysics, could lead to more frightful methods of destruction than atomic energy.

What matters our boasted scientific age if the instruments of science are manned by moral lepers? A sense of moral responsibility and the capacity for moral indignation are the measure of a man. The apparent complete indifference of many youths, teachers, and educated people to any

[1] From "Strictly Personal," *Chicago Daily News.* Used by permission.

clear distinction between right and wrong is amazing. Such moral blindness is suicide in a moral universe. God honors lives built on the rock of righteousness. Lives built on the sands of sin are without foundation. In personal terms this means God is not much interested in how smart we are or in how much money we have. He is interested in how honest, just, loving, truthful, and pure we are.

IV

God measures men by *their persistence in pursuit of an ideal.* Years ago in the back room of an apothecary shop in Delft, Holland, a clerk by the name of Anthon van Leeuwenhoek worked night after night, long after he had closed the store, grinding crude lenses from pieces of glass. It was painstaking, tiresome work. No one before him had ever done it. He then patiently began to examine things under the glass. He looked at the tartar from his teeth, a little rain water, a bit of fish. There he discovered—the first human to see it—the invisible world of the microbes. "He was the only man in the world at that time who believed there were these tiny invisible forms of life." He wrote of his findings to the British Royal Society for the Advancement of Science. But the story was fantastic to the learned men of the time. It was impossible! "They laughed at him, they scorned his ignorance, they chided him for his lack of integrity." Although opposed by the whole scientific world, this drug clerk of Delft persisted in his pursuit of the truth. The truth supported his faithfulness. His discoveries became the very basis of modern medicine.

It is always so. The man who seeks the truth is willing to be patient. The man who is right can afford to wait. The man who is dedicated to a great ideal never gives up. The man who chooses to be on God's side is not afraid to stand alone. Lives that are important by divine measurements are lives that dare to dream and then dare to carry that dream through to the end, in spite of opposition and criticism.

The trouble with most of us is not that we don't dream our dream but that we give up too easily. We lack staying power. We quit growing. We give up trying. We get tired of the weariness and the effort it takes. We shrink from criticism. Our ideal fades. We begin to want things handed to us on a silver platter. We excuse ourselves by heeding the doctrine that we are pawns of fate, and we say, "What's the use anyway?" We take the easy path of least resistance.

However, the business of being a Christian, of being a truth seeker, of believing in freedom, of building a worthy business, of creating a home, of getting an education, of conducting a life, are all lifetime jobs. They last as long as life lasts. Not beginnings but *endings* count! God honors men who never stop growing, never cease trying.

V

God measures men by *their ability to capitalize on adversity*. The title of a book on how to play golf is revealing: *Golf After Forty!* There is an interesting illustration in it that has a good point for us. The author, H. A. Hattstrom, tells of his experience one time in playing the eighteenth hole at the Glencoe, Illinois, Club. The hole is 560 yards and runs due north. On that particular day a stiff north wind was blowing dead against the players. His third shot had a bad pull to the left which gave him a difficult lie behind a high tree, a drinking fountain, and a group of benches. These obstacles made a direct shot to the tee impossible. He was too close to the tree to go over it. Hattstrom decided to use the wind to his advantage. He played a high spin ball directly into the wind and to the side of the tree. He aimed for twenty-five yards away from and beyond the green. When the spin had spent itself, the wind took over and brought the ball back south to the green where it stopped within three feet of the cup. The ball traveled an arc, almost a semicircle. It was an intentional "slice." The author made the point that such a play would have been impossible without the wind. He said that good golfers make use of the wind instead of fighting it.

Life is like that! Every man at times finds himself in a bad lie, with the wind against him. Life deals us hard jolts sometimes. Frequently these are not our fault. In such situations God measures a man by his courage to play into the wind. God wants a man to use unfavorable conditions as an aid instead of a handicap in gaining his objectives. Play in the rough tests the mettle of a golfer. His reactions to the disappointments, heartaches, and failures of life mark the measure of a man in the sight of God. This is a homely truth that is easily forgotten in our age of soft living. The significant goals are never easy to reach. God expects us to attain them, to have the wisdom and courage to play into the wind.

VI

God measures men by *their measurement of him.* A good many years ago a young man in Baltimore started out to make his way in New York. Before he left, he had a talk with a canal boat captain, an old friend of the family. The old man asked him what he could do to make a living. The boy replied that he knew how to make soap and candles. "Do that and do it well," replied the skipper. "And take the Lord into partnership. Give him at least one tenth of what you make, and you will never fail." Before long the boy was managing a New York soap firm. Then he started a little soap business of his own. He always set aside ten cents of each dollar for the church. On his books his donations were marked: "Account with the Lord." As business prospered, he told the bookkeeper to advance that one tenth to two tenths, then to three tenths, then to five tenths. He honored God not only with his money but with his time and influence. He built his life on divine principles and by eternal standards. He recognized God at the center of life, and God honored him, blessed him, and used him in the kingdom. The Baltimore boy who took God into partnership in all his affairs was William Colgate. Soapmaker, yes, but likewise a great Christian layman. He was one of the first directors of the American Bible Society and the man for whom Colgate University was named.

Just because a man gives generously to the church does not mean that he prospers materially. But in the final analysis the true measure of a man is the measure of his recognition of a great God as a partner in the enterprise of living. Most of us limit our own stature by worshiping a limited God in a limited way. Let a man worship a God big enough to be worthy of his highest devotion! Let him put that God at the center of his philosophy of life, at the focus of his personality and career, and his stature will take on new dimensions. He will find new heights and depths to life. He shall be as a giant in the earth. The size, meaning, and worth of the things we worship determine our own size, meaning, and worth. We become great as we worship a great God.

INDEPENDENCE DAY

The American Way

Blessed is the nation whose God is the Lord.
—Ps. 33:12

THE ROMAN EMPIRE BACK IN A.D. 301 WHEN DIOCLETIAN was emperor began a program of state regulation which brought to an end Roman civilization and marked the beginning of the Dark Ages. Prices and wages were controlled by the state. Violations of government orders were punished by banishment or death. Personal freedoms were limited, and the people ceased to work and to exercise their own initiative. During the thousand years that followed, the Roman Empire produced not a single poet, historian, painter, sculptor, or architect of any note. Famines were frequent. In their fight for more food human beings were little better than the beasts of the field.

For an example in recent years the British Empire has been facing a financial crisis that threatens to bankrupt English economy. Further reductions in its already barren standard of living are ahead. One big reason for this condition is that the socialistic programs in England are costing far more than expected and are draining the country beyond endurance. The English people are learning the hard way what Ramsay Macdonald learned. When Ramsay

Macdonald, the first Labor Party member to become Prime Minister of England, was about to enter upon his second term, President Hoover asked him: "Did you learn anything in your first term which will be helpful to you in your second?"

"Yes," said Ramsay Macdonald, "I learned one thing— that you can't make the poor richer by making the rich poorer."

It has been so throughout history. Whenever men deify the state and look to the state for the regulation of life from the cradle to the grave, they are always disappointed. In the end they lose far more than they gain. When men surrender their liberties to the state in search of security, they soon discover that they have given up that security. Security in the last analysis is always based on freedom.

Many Americans today betray their heritage by being afraid of freedom. Freedom has been the single distinguishing feature of American life that has made this nation great. Freedom has made this the one spot on the earth where life is secure and where all people enjoy a reasonable standard of living. Natural resources, climate, hard work, intellectual capacity, and religion have played their part. But freedom is the reason these factors have had their full chance to operate.

It is important for us therefore to celebrate the freedom of the individual in America. He must be free to work out his own destiny in his own way, controlled only by laws to prevent him from interfering with the freedom of others. This simple, basic idea of personal freedom is founded on the Christian idea of God and the sacredness of life. It was released on the scene of history through the Declaration of

Independence. It has given to American life a driving force and has created social progress and achievements unknown before in all the history of mankind. No collectivist or totalitarian state in history has done so much for so many.

Our national freedom is seriously threatened and ridiculed today. Lying Communist propaganda, the programs of a handout state, top-heavy government expenses, and socialistic schemes supported by burdensome and self-defeating taxation—all tend to destroy freedom. In the face of these factors the Christian citizen may well recover his faith in America as a land of opportunity and freedom for the individual. This in turn becomes the basis for personal and national security. It is in an atmosphere of freedom and not regimentation that we can best solve our problems.

I

The American way of freedom is *opportunity regardless of race or color*. Let us consider, in our deep concern for the problems of race discrimination and injustice, the case of Walter Edwards, a successful businessman of Oklahoma City. When he was fourteen, he helped his father on a small farm. He was hardly able to read or write, yet he dreamed of having a business of his own and helping needy people. In 1921 he went to the city and got a job in a junk yard for nine dollars a week. He always managed to save a few cents a week for bigger things. Two years later he bought a horse and wagon and went in the junk business himself. Out of every dollar he still saved for the future. Sometime later he bought the Minor Baggage and Transfer Company. Then he bought into the Economy Carpet Cleaners and the Enterprise Iron Foundry.

In 1931 Walter married a young woman who knew something about bookkeeping. She helped him straighten out his tangled acounts. Then he went into the construction business. Some years later he built the "Edwards Addition" in Oklahoma City, a housing development of five hundred homes for Negroes in moderate circumstances. The Edwardses were very happy. Then Mrs. Edwards became sick and went to the Mayo Clinic for treatment. While there she began thinking about the poorer people who could not afford hospital care. Soon she and her husband began planning a hospital. Today the Edwards Memorial Hospital of 105 beds is serving everyone regardless of creed, race, or color. Frances and Walter Edwards contributed most of the funds. The dreams of a farm boy came true. It's a familiar story in America. The interesting thing about it is that Frances and Walter Edwards are Negroes living in a country in which many would have us believe Negroes are not supposed to have a chance.

That's the American way of solving the race problem. This is not an isolated case. There are many instances of others achieving success. Paul Robeson may long for Russia as a land of opportunity for the Negro. There are many who feel that he, and other Negroes who feel as he does, should live there. But Walter Edwards and thousands of others prefer the good old U.S.A. in spite of its shortcomings, as a place for the kind of opportunity that means most. We deplore the discrimination in Washington, D.C., that prevented Ralph Bunche from accepting the post as Assistant Secretary of State. However, Dr. Bunche should not forget the freedoms of American life which enabled him to develop himself into the most distinguished Negro of the country. God knows we have a long way to go and have made many mistakes. But we can go farther as a free state than as a slave state in the solution of the problems of race.

II

The American way of freedom is *opportunity regardless of age.* Many say that young men don't have a chance in America any more. We hear that everything has already been done, that there are no new frontiers to challenge youth in the American system. This philosophy is more dangerous than any communist attack. On the initiative and courage and ambition of youth depend the future of the country.

All you need to do is to take a look at the list of the ten outstanding young men in the nation recently selected by the U.S. Junior Chamber of Commerce. There is Sidney S. McMath, 36, governor of Arkansas, selected for his fight as a prosecuting attorney in ending the twenty-year control of a Hot Springs political machine, and for setting an example to young men in public service.

There is Dr. Charles A. Hufnagle, 32, instructor in surgery at Harvard Medical School, selected for the development of new surgical techniques and the establishment of artery banks.

There is Richard N. Harris, 33, of St. Paul, who created a new industry and a business worth twenty million dollars in four years from an original investment of a thousand dollars.

Mike Gorman, 34, newspaper reporter, was selected for

exposing conditions in Oklahoma's mental institutions which resulted in a model mental health act.

Frank P. Zeidler, 36, mayor of Milwaukee, was selected for outstanding advancements in municipal government.

If you think thirty is too ripe an age, consider Nancy Rowe, 16, who works in her father's grocery store. Nancy made a thinner-than-hair microneedle for injecting chemicals into living cells. This technic may contribute toward finding a cure for cancer. Or take Doris Pines, 18, who has composed music played and praised by Stokowski. Or there is Andres Kende, who at 15 is developing a way to reduce or remove explosion hazards in chemical synthesis.

Let no one say that America is old, washed up, exhausted; that her young people are facing blind alleys. Let no one say that free enterprise has run its course, that it is foolish to take any more chances, to dream any more dreams. America is the one country where youth may yet dare to venture and hope and plan and work with a real chance to win.

III

The American way is the way of *opportunity regardless of nationality, religion, or condition of life.* The idea that the American laboring man is a poor, downtrodden creature suffering under the capitalistic heel of oppression is an absurdity. To say that the little man hasn't a chance any more is absolutely untrue.

The story of Sou Chan, formerly of Yingping, Canton Province, China, is remarkable. Chan came to this country in 1927 a young man and a complete stranger. In 1935 he went to New York and got a job driving a truck. Although frail of build, he drove the truck for three years, often sleeping in it to save his money. By hard work and rigid economy he had saved enough in three years to make the down payment on a small restaurant. As his character and credit became sufficiently established, he was able to borrow a little to expand. The House of Chan, as it is called now, is worth over a quarter of a million dollars. Sou Chan, Chinese Buddhist, immigrant truck driver, lives in a $50,000 house in Riverdale, drives a Cadillac, and winters in Florida. He married an American-born Chinese girl from Boston and numbers among his personal friends prominent Jewish, Catholic, Chinese, and Protestant people.

You might tell some college graduates that nobody has a chance in America any more without a pull. Many believe that the little man never gets anywhere. But don't tell Sou Chan that! The trouble with too many of our graduates is that they want to begin at the top.

And don't tell that to Chief Justice Fred M. Vinson or Justice William O. Douglas; or to Governors Thomas E. Dewey and Earl Warren; or to Bing Crosby and Bob Hope; or to Charles Luckman, former president of Lever Brothers; or to Senators Wayne Morse or Robert Wagner. They all began as newsboys and worked their way to the top. In spite of its detractors and belittlers, America is still the land of opportunity. The little man in America, no matter what his status, is far better off in liberties and goods than his counterpart in any collectivist state.

IV

The American way is the way of *opportunity regardless of handicaps and difficulty*. We want things handed to us

109

on a silver platter. When conditions are difficult, we look to the government for help in business, education, medicine, housing. It is high time we learned again to stand on our own feet and fight our own battles even when the odds are against us.

Take the case of Bonifacio Yturbide, who graduated not long ago from the University of Nevada. He had all A's in all courses in all four years, the highest record in the history of the school. He won the Herz Gold Medal, the university's highest scholastic honor. He was popular in the school, the star of the debating team, and a fine chess player. In high-school days in Reno he had likewise made straight A's and was president of his senior class. He won one of 117 university scholarships competing nationally with 14,000 students. Bonafacio's case is interesting because he is the son of Basque immigrants and a severe illness at the age of three left him totally blind.

Here is a fine example of the American spirit to tackle a tough situation and see it through with courage and faith. How we need this spirit today! When prices are down from all-time peaks, we head for the storm cellar and say a depression is on. When employment is off from all-time highs, we begin to want the government to make jobs. Business in America suffers from a fear phobia. When times get harder, we need more faith as an antidote to fear. Government collectivism may look good, but it is deadly. It takes out some things very vital to the American character: personal initiative, ingenuity, ambition. We cry for security when what we really need is freedom. We need freedom from the superstate, freedom to pit the minds and energies of free men against the problems of life. We need freedom to create, to improve, to sell, to compete. With that freedom America's future is unlimited.

"The solution of America's problem is not in terms of big government nor big labor nor big business but it is in big men over whom nobody stands in control but God." Exactly so! And this is the core of the whole matter. For this concept of freedom is based on the recognition of Almighty God as the supreme ruler of men. The Declaration of Independence and the Constitution were based on this fundamental idea. Long ago William Penn said, "Unless we are governed by God, we will be governed by tyrants." The chief aid of free men in their resistance to the tyranny of the superstate is their worship of God, their recognition of the Christian principles at the heart of life. The temptation to make the state a god is appealing but dangerous to freedom. The welfare state easily becomes the collectivist state. The collectivist state becomes the police state. The police state becomes the totalitarian state.

So it is that Independence Day is a good time for us Christians to examine our freedoms. We do well to declare again our faith in God, in the individual, and in freedom as the supports basic to peace and national security.

LABOR DAY

The Gospel of Labor

Workers together with him.
—II Cor. 6:1

ONE OF THE GLORIOUS THINGS ABOUT THE MASTER WAS THAT he was a *worker*. Whereas most founders of religions lived lives of contemplation and ease, Jesus worked with his hands. He did not complain about his lot or feel down-trodden because of it. He was proud of his work. He thus dignified the labor of men as a vital part of the program of God for humankind.

This is the gospel of labour, ring it, ye bells of the kirk!
The Lord of Love came down from above, to live with the men
who work.
This is the rose that He planted, here in the thorn-curst soil:
Heaven is blest with perfect rest, but the blessing of Earth is
toil.[1]

Let us consider, then, three implications of this Christian gospel of labor.

I

Work is *an instrument of the good and full life*. Robert Gibbings in *Lovely Is the Lee* tells the tale of an old man

[1] From "The Toiling of Felix," *The Poems of Henry van Dyke,* published by Chas. Scribner's Sons. Used by permission.

with two lazy sons. He had not been able to get them to work. They had been waiting for him to die to get his money. Before he died, he told them that there was a crock of gold buried in one of the fields not more than eighteen inches beneath the surface. When the old man had gone, the sons began to dig furiously. They dug in deep furrows over every inch of the field for fear of missing it. They never could find it, and their grass field was ruined. They decided there was nothing to do but sow the field in oats. The money they made from the oats was worth more than any crock of gold. Moreover, they learned the priceless lesson of work which their father had intended they should learn. Too many people these days are trying to find a pot of gold without working for it.

We need to recover a sense of the importance of honest, plain, hard work as the basis of our economic life. It is the keystone of our national character. It is also a tonic for living at its best. Furthermore, we need to recover a sense of pride of workmanship. The shoddy worker is a liability to himself and society. It is work well done that makes men happy, creative, useful, and leads to life's highest rewards of satisfaction. The gold-brickers, the lazy, idle people, the careless workers, are the most bored, unhappy people on earth. They are their own enemies.

It is not the kind or amount of work but our attitude toward it that determines the effect on us. One attitude is represented in a statement of Oscar Wilde:

There is nothing necessarily dignified about labor at all, and most of it is absolutely degrading. To sweep a slushy crossing for eight hours a day when the east wind is blowing is a disgusting occupation. To sweep it with mental, moral, or physical dig-

113

nity seems to me utterly impossible. Man is made for something better than disturbing the dirt.

Another and more healthy attitude toward work is represented by Tony Ridando, who showed up one night on the late Major Bowes's famous radio amateur hour. The major asked him what he did. "Me, I work on a garbage wagon; I collecta da garbage."

Said the major, "You collect garbage, Tony. Why that's pretty hard work, isn't it? Pretty bad work, too."

Replied Tony, "Oh, I notta so sure, Mister Major. Maybe. But anyway, it maka me a good living for twelve year now."

Then Tony burst into a tenor aria from *Rigoletto* in a voice clear and joyous. Tony, the garbage collector, was Antonio the King. The menial was at home in company with the gods. The applause was deafening in honor, not of a great singer, but of a humble, honest worker.

Aye, let no man be ashamed to work if he does his job well, if he is working for some greater objective than the satisfaction of his own personal physical desires. "Man shall not live by bread alone." (Matt. 4:4.) A full dinner pail is no assurance of a full life. We must see beyond our work its true meaning; then we find even the plainest jobs not only bearable but a source of satisfaction and joy. God made men not for idleness and pleasure alone but for toil and labor. Work makes for strong, sturdy, self-reliant personalities. Work makes us stable, self-respecting citizens. Work relieves the pressures of boredom, phobias, memories. Work leads to thrift and security. Thank God for it!

II

Work has an important place in our American life and economy. All fair-minded men recognize the place of labor in the building of the nation. We are glad to honor the working man and are concerned with his improvement. What the laboring man needs to recognize now, however, is that his welfare depends on the welfare of the total country, including management and government. The American laborer must refuse to weep over his so-called downtrodden status as his communist exploiters would have him to do. Instead he should rejoice in his place as the envy of the working men of the world.

In the past six generations this nation has made more progress in terms of living standards than all other nations combined have made in six thousand years. A hundred years ago the average factory worker worked seventy hours a week, and machines did 6 per cent of the work. Today he works forty hours, and machines do 85 per cent of the work. He makes more per hour than he formerly got per day. Moreover, machines have created more jobs, not fewer. In 1890, 29 per cent of our population was gainfully employed; today, 43 per cent. The worker is way ahead in spite of inflation. During the peak of the inflation years the Department of Labor said that the earnings of U.S. factory workers had risen 107 per cent in the previous eight years. This should be compared with a 61 per cent rise in the cost of living for the same period.

The average American worker is far better off than he admits. A man had a combination chauffeur and yard man working for him who attended communist meetings frequently. Then he quit going, and his boss asked why.

"At the last meeting it was proved that if the wealth of the country was divided equally, each person would have $2,000," he replied.

"So what?" asked his boss.

"Well, I have $5,000 now!"

The American laborer needs to renounce the vicious hold of communist leaders who victimize labor's rank and file by promising utopias that never can be realized. They hold out only slavery in exchange for freedom. The collectivist state is a slave state and the enemy of free labor. American labor must renounce the leadership of hoodlums, racketeers, and gangsters whose grafting, chiseling, thieving, and mobster tactics are a disgrace to honest American labor. American labor must renounce inexcusable practices used to hamper production, slow down work, encourage shoddy workmanship, protect incompetents, and discredit American enterprise. American management and labor both need to recognize that they are dependent on each other. Only as they co-operate in their joint enterprise can we have a still greater America, free, secure, democratic, strong. The challenge of Russian Communism to the economy of America cannot be met by cringing crooks and crackpots crying about their abused rights. No more can it be met by greedy industrialists without conscience or social vision. It can be met only by free, intelligent men with a high sense of responsibility and partnership in a great enterprise for the future of the nation. If we all work together, a civilization can be established such as few men have ever dreamed possible.

There is a fable about a man who lived long ago with two wives. He was middle-aged. One wife was old, and the other young. This man was getting gray-haired. The young wife did not like that, so while he was asleep, she pulled out his gray hairs. The older wife liked for him to appear older and nearer her own age; therefore she pulled out his black hairs. Soon the poor man was bald.

Our economy is going to be in just that bald a state so long as every group takes out only that which serves its own interest. Those who work and those who manage, those who own and those who consume, those who grow crops and those who govern people, must recognize that the interest of each is bound up with the interest of all.

Jesus recognized the dissimilar talents of men and rewarded them accordingly. Nowhere did he try to reduce all men to the same level. He was no belligerent laborer with an exaggerated class consciousness. He is today allied with all who build creatively, with muscle, mind, and money. He would inspire men to work together so that they might realize the highest in them as the children of God.

III

The work of man is related to the work of God. Perhaps we have all felt that religion spent a large portion of its force in doing things apart from life: sacrificing, prayers, travels to Mecca, Jerusalem, Rome; kissing sacred stones, climbing sacred stairs, bathing in sacred waters. But we need to see that any useful work, done honestly and with a vision of its end purpose, may be a token of our partnership with God.

After all, though God made the forests, he did not make the gardens. He made the quarries, but not the cathedrals.

117

He made the herbs, but not the medicines. We are apt to think that the only way we can serve God is to go to church, teach a class, or sing in the choir. But God needs the daily work of man if his will is to be accomplished upon the earth. And all useful work is important.

The story is told of a man who went to an employment bureau to register for work. The clerk said, "Can you mow lawns, type, raise chickens, keep books, lay bricks, teach, cook, sew, sell shoes, keep bees, wash windows, saw wood, write, dig ditches, run a comptometer, paint pictures, build bridges, proofread, orate, milk, grow bananas, do janitor work, run a jackhammer, drive a truck, wax floors, wait tables, wash cars, make paper flowers, plaster, prescribe medicines, pile coal, lay sidewalks, solder metals, manage a store, doctor trees, carry a hod, take care of children, or slaughter steers?"

"Yes," said the man.

"Sorry, no openings," said the clerk. Strangely enough, however, God can use us all. Whether we grow bananas or paint pictures, he has openings for each one of us in his great workshop. It is when men learn to do their work in partnership with God and honor him in their tasks that the world will be redeemed from its crassness, meanness, greed, and bitter strife.

Donald Fraser tells of a very religious elder of a Glasgow church. He taught Sunday school, preached in outdoor meetings, and served the church in many other ways. He was a baker by trade. One day on a train he was accosted by a zealous lady passenger who asked him if he was a Christian. When he replied in the affirmative, she asked him what work he did for the Master. "I bake," he said.

"Ah, I did not ask you about your trade, but what service do you give to him who redeemed you?"

"Madam, I bake."

She was nettled but persisted. "I mean how are you seeking to glorify Christ and spread his gospel?"

Again his only reply was, "I bake."

He was a wise Scotsman. For a true conception of Christianity makes common things holy and in daily service finds the greatest expression of a life's devotion. We Americans need to rededicate the labor of our hands and the tasks of our lives to the service of God. That way lies the coming of the kingdom.

Henry Ward Beecher said one time, "Religion means work. Religion means work in a dirty world. Religion means peril; blows given but blows taken as well. Religion means transformation. The world is to be cleaned by somebody, and you are not called of God if you are ashamed to scour and scrub."

There are strange ways of serving God;
You sweep a room or turn a sod,
And suddenly, to your surprise,
You hear the whirr of seraphim,
And find you're under God's own eyes
And building palaces for Him.[2]

[2] Hermann Hagedorn, "Service." Used by permission.

119

The Hope of the World

That they all may be one; . . . that the world may believe that thou hast sent me.

—John 17:21

THE NIGHT OF THE FIRST RAID ON LONDON'S EAST END IN September, 1940, the London newspaper editors were concerned about how the raids would affect the morale of the people. They held a meeting that night and agreed among themselves to appeal to the heroic in the English people. Next morning the newspapers carried all the stories they could of bravery, courage, sacrifice, patience, and service during the raids. Said one of the editors: "Right then and there we fixed the pattern of how people ought to behave in an air raid."

To Christians of the world this World Communion Sunday may well set a pattern of fellowship and faith that shall be to all men a guide and beacon in a darkened time.

I

World Communion symbolizes *the world-wide fellowship of the Christian faith*. Kenneth Scott Latourette, of Yale, said of Christianity: "Never before in the history of the race has any group of ideas, religious, social, economic, or political, been propagated over so wide an area or among so many people by so many who have given their lives to the task."

Today therefore we rejoice that we are attached to no petty event, no localized endeavor, no restricted company. We are lured again by the epic quality of a drama with a stage as wide as the world of men. This gospel of ours knows no iron curtain of economic system or political order. It crosses every frontier of geography and flows over every barrier of color, class, and culture.

The gospel hymns are sung with equal fervor by Eskimos and Fiji Islanders, in a Park Avenue cathedral and in an African hut. The Bible is translated into almost every known tongue. "Come unto me" and "I am the way" are read with reverence in Chinese and Russian. Christian spires are found from Madagascar to Maine, from Bombay to Brazil. The old, old story finds responsive hearts among wastrels of Hell's Kitchen and the lepers of Molokai. At hospitals, orphanages, and schools the world around, the sun never sets on the Christian flag. In Berlin, Rio de Janeiro, Stockholm, Tokyo, and Nome Christians gather for the Lord's Supper. Humbly and with a deep sense of gratitude and respect therefore we today share in the only true world family. In a very real sense this is the hope of the world. We acknowledge God as Father of all. We pledge help to those in need, our brothers for whom Christ died. We offer our support to all who seek to live as Christians.

II

World Communion symbolizes *the centrality of Christ* in the redemption of human life and the life of the world. Arthur Brisbane said:

We may sweep the world clean of militarism. We may scrub the world white of autocracy. We may carpet it with democracy. . . . We may spend energy and effort to make the world a Paradise itself, where the lion of capitalism can lie down with the proletarian lamb. But if we turn into that splendid room mankind with the same old heart, "deceitful and desperately wicked," we may expect to clean house again not many days hence. What we need is a peace conference with the Prince of Peace.

Exactly so! Therefore at the Communion table we subscribe to no mere ideology. We acknowledge rather the lordship of a life that is above every life. There can be no Christianity without Christ. All cults, sects, religions, and philosophies, however lofty, are pale and impotent before the Christ. We worship not a beautiful ideal or an abstract truth or a diluted, vague, disembodied idea. We worship the historical Jesus, the son of God, the crucified Lord of mankind. He is our Saviour, our Redeemer, our Master. It is well for us to quit skirting the edge of life and come face to face with Jesus. It is then our brazen excuses give way, our smug defenses crumble, our callous hearts meet defeat.

Christ's truth is the final truth. God is Father. Life is sacred and good. Love and service are the bases of human relations. Men are brothers. Right and freedom are eternal values. This is God's world, and God's word is in it. Aye, there is no name given by which men may be saved save this name. In Christ we find life that is life eternal; through him forgiveness of God; with him renewal of spirit.

Christ's love is the only power holy enough to redeem the race. Here is a love that sees all men as equal in God's sight. Here is a love that is strong enough to suffer on a cross for the sin of men. Here is a love that is powerful enough to redeem men from the savagery and brutality that clutch at the heart of the race. In Christ we find rest for weary lives and salvation for soiled souls. In him we find the challenge to save our world from destruction by evil men.

Christ's program is the only program possible for human society. We can't have a world at all unless it is a Christian world. In vain do we look to scientific inventions, economic agreements, political arrangements, for salvation. In Christ alone is the hope of the world.

III

World Communion symbolizes *the growing unity of the Christian conscience, voice, and church.* The growing unity of Protestant Christendom, dramatized by the great World Council of Churches session at Amsterdam, is expressed vividly in this section from the council's message to the churches:

We are divided from one another not only in matters of faith, order, and tradition, but also by pride of nation, class, and race. But Christ has made us His own, and He is not divided. In seeking Him we find one another. . . .

Our coming together to form a World Council will be vain unless Christians and Christian congregations everywhere commit themselves to the Lord of the Church in a new effort to seek together, where they live, to be his witnesses and servants among their neighbours. . . . We have to make of the Church in every place a voice for those who have no voice, and a home where every man will be at home. . . . We have to ask God to teach us together to say "No" . . . to all that flouts the love of Christ, to every system, every programme, and every person

123

that treats any man as though he were an irresponsible thing or a means of profit, to the defenders of injustice in the name of order, to those who sow the seeds of war or urge war as inevitable; "Yes" to all that conforms to the love of Christ, to all who seek for justice, to the peacemakers, to all who hope, fight, and suffer for the cause of man. . . .

It is not in man's power to banish sin and death from the earth, to create the unity of the Holy Catholic Church, to conquer the hosts of Satan. But it is within the power of God.

Well, thank God Christians are moving together!

Yes, this solemn sacrament symbolizes the unity and deepens the fellowship which the disciples of Christ enjoy as members of his body the Church. We are not alone! We get strength at this table from millions who share this sacrament and share the redemptive plan of God.

REFORMATION SUNDAY

What Protestants Believe

He is the head of the body, the church.
—Col. 1:18

THE ROMAN CATHOLIC CHURCH IS MAKING A STRONG BID
for power in the United States. One part of its program
consists of a series of large newspaper advertisements con-
taining statements of Catholic faith and practice. These
boldly challenge Protestant views and positions. It becomes
increasingly important therefore for Protestants to know
more of their own beliefs. Protestant Reformation Sunday
affords a good opportunity to restate the Protestant faith
against the background of Roman Catholic ideas.

I

Protestants believe that the *Bible* and not the church is
the *supreme authority* for the Christian. One of the Catholic
advertisements carried this comment about the text: "And I
say to thee; that thou art Peter, and upon THIS rock will
I build my church. And the gates of hell shall not prevail
against it." It states:

Surely, if the Son of God meant what he said, He had founded
only one Church for the salvation of all men . . . and the head
of that Church was obviously St. Peter, the first Pope of the Holy

Roman Catholic Church. To that Church . . . *and that Church alone* . . . Christ had given the keys of the kingdom of heaven. To that Church—and that Church alone—Christ had given the power to bind and loose . . . to forgive or deny forgiveness.[1]

Another advertisement quotes Pope Pius IX as follows:

We must hold . . . that out of the Apostolic Roman Catholic Church there is no salvation; that She is the only ark of safety, and whosoever is not in Her perishes in the deluge. . . . All of God's grace is distributed through the Catholic Church.

The Protestant, however, denies that the church—any church, whatever its origin or claims—is the final authority for religious truth, the exclusive channel of the mind of God and the Spirit of Jesus. Indeed such claims are in no way in keeping with the teachings of Jesus, with the universal fatherhood of God, or with any reasonable conception of divine truth. Jesus put no such test of an exclusive Church before men as a requirement of discipleship. For Christ fellowship in the kingdom of love and the blessing of eternal life depended on qualities of the mind, heart, and life. Salvation did not depend on membership in this or that organization, or on magical rites and ceremonies. There was nothing in the attitude of Jesus to give the spirit of exclusiveness to his disciples. His mind would revolt against the quibbling over technicalities indulged in so freely by his would-be followers.

The life and teachings of Jesus are the original source of the Christian program. This means that the Bible naturally becomes for the Protestant believer the supreme moral and spiritual authority for human life. The Bible existed in

[1] *St. Louis Post-Dispatch,* Sept. 23, 1944.

manuscript form even before it was brought together in the present form, and has been the basis of spiritual strength through the centuries. The only time the Bible has failed men has been when it has been kept from the people. The leaders of certain churches always have been afraid of what it would mean for their exclusive religious empires.

Even here, however, Protestants do not claim an external, mechanical authority for the Bible or that all of it is equally fruitful for divine instruction. The authority of the Bible comes from its own gift of spiritual power to men. It does not come from any set of theological beliefs or interpretations thereof by any church.

The Bible is supreme in its authority because of what it does for us. It sets a divine worth on the individual. It puts sinful men in touch with the redeeming love of God. It reveals the moral judgment of God that no enduring civilization can be built on foundations of hatred, greed, and force. It reveals a satisfying and life-transforming source of divine power and peace adaptable to the needs of all men.

The Bible is supreme for the Protestant because it puts Christ supreme. Its climactic message for men is that Christ is the head of the Church. For any church to say that it alone is the exclusive channel of God's salvation is to do strong violence to the ablest scholarship of free minds. The intelligent common sense of millions of high-minded men declares this untrue. The most enlightened movements of human history deny it. The witness of generations of faithful and humble believers as well as the spirit of the Master testify to the contrary. The finest spiritual feelings of men

127

declare the absurdity of this position. No earthly creature, past or present, dare seek to supplant the divine Christ as the great head of the Church.

II

Protestants believe in *the right of the individual to interpret the Scriptures.* To quote another of the advertisements:

If Christ meant what He said . . . and who could doubt that He did? . . . He certainly meant that He was establishing one particular Church for the salvation of all men. He certainly meant that *that* church was the Holy Roman Catholic Church. . . . What good then to seek salvation elsewhere? What good to read the Bible, to sing the praises of the Savior, to admit that salvation is possible only through Christ?

All of this, of course, cuts across the belief of the Protestant in the right of private judgment and the right of a free choice of worship. Indeed the right of private judgment is one of the most basic and essential beliefs of Protestantism. The Protestant position asserts that the individual child of God has the God-given right to find for himself the light and life of the Gospels. He is individually responsible to God for his own salvation.

The attempt of any church group to maintain an exclusive right to interpret the Scriptures is a dangerous threat to religious freedom. This was the cause of the corruption of the early church which makes such unpleasant chapters in early European and Italian history.

The attempt of any church to discredit or belittle the Bible does a disservice to the total cause of religion, undermines American democracy and has no support in human experience. For the hungry hearts of men have found eternal life direct from its pages without the permission or censorship of holy men.

Another of the advertisements has this to say:

They have even accused various Popes of the Catholic Church of suppressing the Bible, without the trouble to include in their accusations the fact that these condemned versions [i.e. the Protestant Bible] were not faithful copies of the Bible itself, but deliberate mistranslations published to support false religious teachings. . . . The Catholic Church is the Mother of the Bible. The only assurance you have that the Bible contains the word of God is the assurance given you by the Catholic Church.[2]

The facts are to the contrary. The open Bible, accessible to the humblest of men, freely interpreted by the common man, has been the basis of democracy and human progress. Make no mistake about that.

Hear John Ruskin, the father of modern social reform: "Everything I have ever written, every greatness that has been in any thought of mine, whatever I have done in my life has been simply due to the fact that, when I was a child, my mother daily read with me a part of the Bible and daily made me learn a part of it by heart."

Hear Theodore Roosevelt: "Almost every man who has by his lifework added to the sum of human achievement has based his lifework upon the teachings of the Bible."

Hear Woodrow Wilson: "A man has deprived himself of the best there is in the world who has deprived himself of a knowledge of the Bible."

Hear Andrew Jackson: "The Bible is the rock on which our Republic rests."

True, this freedom of interpretation makes for divisions

[2] *St. Louis Post-Dispatch,* Oct. 28, 1944.

among Protestant sects. This is Protestantism's glory, for the Protestant Church does not try to pour all men's minds into one mold. Moreover such divisions are not exclusive to Protestantism. Rather divisions in freedom, however, than unity under fear!

The Protestant holds that here in the pages of this Book, so plain a child can find it, is the bread of life, strength for the burdened, healing and peace for the grieved, salvation for the sinful. It calls to the divinity within us, gives us the long view, releases us from the paralysis of fear, hate, and bigotry.

III

Protestants believe that salvation comes *by faith in God through Christ* and not from any human authority or intermediary. The Protestant puts the individual conscience above submission to external human authority in any form or organization. The Protestant makes the inner attitude of the soul more important than ritual.

The Roman Catholic Church puts itself between man and God. Said another of the advertisements:

Christ empowered Catholic priests not merely to *announce* that sins were forgiven, but actually to *forgive* sins. And notice too that He did not tell them to forgive or refuse forgiveness indiscriminately, but according to their judgment of the just deserts of the sinner. And finally, note that this authority is not confined to any particular kind of sins, but extends to all sins without exception.

The Protestant believes, on the other hand, that the individual himself stands before God and does business with God. He believes that only God forgives sin through the

grace of his Son Jesus Christ. He is profoundly grateful
that the forgiveness of his sins is not dependent on the
whimsey and fallibility of human judgment.

This whole conception of salvation finds its finest expression
in the cardinal doctrine of Paul, justification by faith.
Paul rebelled against the idea that men could be saved by
some outward ceremony, by some measure of good work,
or by some mechanical religious rite. His witness to the
direct power of God operative in human lives has been
the inspiration of countless Christians through the ages.

This Protestant principle of individual justification by
faith—direct with God—has been at the basis of religious
freedom. It puts the eternal welfare of man beyond the
reach of all human tyranny. As such it is the basis of
democracy. Autocratic governments and autocratic churches
go hand in hand. If they become joined, history records
that the common man is held in subjection and ignorance.

IV

Protestants believe in *the sacredness of all life.* We do
not believe in the infallibility of holy men. We do not look
upon the church as an island of holiness in a sea of sinful
men to whom it offers haven and rescue for a consideration.
The Protestant Church holds that there is a universal
priesthood of believers. Protestants regard with equal sanctity
the various kinds of everyday work to which men are
called. The Protestant faith would break down the wall
between the sacred and secular, and put back of the daily
and essential tasks of men a sense of sanctity and moral
worth otherwise reserved for the church. I have no objection
to tipping my hat to a church, but by the same token

I should also want to tip my hat to a hospital, a public school, a farmer tilling the soil, or a Christian home.

This point of the sacredness of the common life is historically important because it was against the gross prostitution of the claims of exclusive holiness that the Protestant Reformation came into being. In a word the Protestant Church came into being because the Roman Catholic Church was morally bankrupt.

This point is important today because it is the basis of our Protestant belief that we are able to govern ourselves in America without dictation from any foreign agency. It is the basis of our Protestant belief that public education is essential to democracy. It is the basis of our willingness as Protestants to co-operate with all men of good will, whatever their religious brand, for the common welfare.

This is no time to exaggerate religious differences in America. Protestants have no desire or intention of starting religious quarrels. Protestants stand solidly on the American tradition of religious freedom. There is a bigger issue than religious freedom at stake in the country today. That is a philosophy of pagan secularism which is the common enemy of all decent people and all churches. Surely if ever in our history, now is the time for all Americans who believe in God and humanity, in goodness and peace, to forget their differences and unite hand and heart against the hate and sin of men. In such an enterprise Protestants are the first to extend the hand of fellowship.

TEMPERANCE WEEK

Men of Distinction

Wine is a mocker, strong drink is raging: and whosoever is deceived thereby is not wise.

—Prov. 20:1

WHEN PRESIDENT FRANKLIN D. ROOSEVELT ANNOUNCED TO the people of the nation the repeal of the Eighteenth Amendment, he used eloquent words to assure us that there would be no recurrence of the evils of public drinking and the open saloon such as existed prior to prohibition. The liquor industry made similar assurances. The extent to which these solemn promises have been broken is all too evident in the "Skid Rows" of America.

Our "Skid Rows" are of course only symptomatic of an increasing public cancer which is steadily eating away at the vitals of our society, namely, the liquor traffic itself. In all of the discussions of the subject little effort is made to come to grips with the real issue, the issue of alcoholic beverages. It is not alcoholism but alcohol that is at the heart of the problem.

Of course there are wide differences of opinion and practice among good, conscientious church people on the question of drinking. I speak without apology, however. The moral, social and personality issues involved deeply concern the kingdom of God. However I object seriously to the manufactured sentiment that this matter is a great sacred cow, against which if anyone lifts a questioning voice he is branded as a long-haired reformer or a bluenose kill-joy.

Since the liquor trade has made the phrase "Men of Distinction" a sort of password and symbol of its lying propaganda, it will be interesting to use it as the basis of a realistic and factual examination of the present status of beverage alcohol in the country.

I

Men of real distinction should be intelligent enough to be *governed by the facts*. It is difficult to understand how hard-headed businessmen who are so carefully concerned about such matters as costs, balance sheets, production schedules, profits, and taxes have such an enormous blind spot when it comes to admitting the heavy burden of alcoholic beverages on our economy and man power. It is not the moralists or preachers to whom they should listen but their own kind.

The Department of Commerce in June, 1948, reported that Americans are spending for alcoholic beverages a total of $9,600,000,000 annually, an average of $26,300,000 a day, a family average of $253. This is $6,000,000,000 in excess of the 1939 figures or almost three times as much. This sum would have built 960,000 new homes at an average price of $10,000, or would have fed 25,000,000 of the world's hungry for a year. This means that on the one hand the normal retail trades in America—food, clothing, furniture—were victimized by this amount, and on the other hand the tax burden of crime, accidents, and inefficiency was correspondingly increased. Our economy loses both ways.

As for the boasted tax return on this spending the American Businessmen's Research Foundation estimates that the total liquor cost to the public is $90 per capita, whereas the tax return in all forms is only $18 per capita.

Bruce Ashby, former official of the Department of Justice, declared at the Industrial Conference on Alcoholism in Chicago that there is a total known loss to industry due to actual alcoholism alone of 28,600,000 work days per year or a cash loss of over $1,000,000,000.

The cost of alcohol to a given state was last analyzed in Massachusetts by a commission headed by Hon. J. T. Zottoli, associate justice of the Boston Municipal Court. It showed that 50 per cent of the felonies and 85 per cent of the misdemeanors are due to alcohol. Insanity caused by alcohol costs the state $4,000,000 a year; crime caused by alcohol cost $6,000,000 a year; the cost of financial dependence on charity caused by alcohol was $51,000,000 a year; chronic alcoholism costs $61,000,000 a year or 4½ times the revenue from liquor taxes.

It has been estimated that the total cost of liquor since repeal of prohibition is equal to the entire wealth of the nation.

The F.B.I. reports show far more arrests for drunkenness than from any other one cause, and state that liquor is the major police problem of America. Mayor Kennelly reported in 1948 that 80 per cent of all cases sent to the Chicago lockup involve alcohol. Superior Court Judge John A. Sbarbaro of Chicago said: "Seventy-five per cent of all the divorce cases I have heard resulted from alcohol." Dr.

Ralph S. Banay, one of the leading criminologists of America, stated: "The majority of sexual crimes are committed under the influence of alcohol." The National Safety Council reported that almost one fourth of all traffic accidents are due to alcohol and cost us $440,000,000 annually. In June and July of 1949 Judge Frank H. Myers in Washington, D.C., tried 3,936 cases involving intoxicated people, an average of 64 a day. Judge Myers appealed in vain for government action of some sort. To our shame Washington, D.C., the capital of our nation, has the highest per capita alcohol consumption in the country. It is a tragedy that the major decisions of our nation come from a city of alcohol-soaked minds.

The final report from the Los Angeles grand jury for 1948 stated: "Our jails and prisons are crowded; our courts and police organizations are burdened; our law enforcement and social welfare problems are seriously aggravated— [all] because of the licensed liquor traffic. The tax costs now falling on the innocent citizenry because of the liquor traffic are intolerable."

There are other facts. Haven Emerson, professor of public health administration at Columbia University, former commissioner of the Board of Health of New York, reports: "Medical sciences have learned and found that alcohol is not a food, a stimulant, nor is it hurtful only in drunkenness. . . . We have learned that alcohol, as commonly used today, causes more disease, disability, and death than any other cause of ill health which is in the power of the individual to prevent and avoid."

The Mayo Clinic has recently stated that the use of

alcohol for medical purposes is out of date and unnecessary with the coming of penicillin and the sulfa drugs.

A twenty-three-year study of 2,000,000 policy holders in forty-three insurance companies was made to determine the effects of alcohol on insurance rates. It showed that the death rate for even moderate drinkers was 186 to 100—or nearly twice as great as for the nondrinkers.

The evidence is overwhelming that in every facet of our economy, industry, home, courts, health, and government beverage alcohol is a costly and damaging influence. It makes no one single constructive, useful, or necessary contribution to our society. Its balance sheet is in the red on every count. What is to be the attitude of the man of distinction to that? It doesn't matter what one's private opinion or habit may be about drinking, the liquor traffic is a major social and economic problem. For true men of distinction to be smugly indifferent to that problem is to court disaster. A nation that spends $3,000,000 a day for education and $24,000,000 a day for alcoholic drinks is going to reap what it sows.

II

Men of real distinction should be independent enough to *resist high pressure, commercialized propaganda, and social custom.* In December, 1948, three Rutgers University sociologists reported in the *Quarterly Journal of Studies on Alcohol* the results of a study of the drinking habits of a large cross section of people. It showed that 43 per cent admitted that they drank for reasons of sociability alone. "I don't like to be a poor sport." "Just to be a good fellow." "Just to be sociable." "I don't care for it at all. I just choke

137

it down." "Our friends drink." "I have to drink as a business courtesy."

In other words almost half of drinking is admittedly due solely to social custom, a custom which has been deliberately cultivated by the liquor industry. Over $100,000,000 a year is spent by the liquor trade in clever advertising adroitly and expertly encouraging the belief that drinking is a normal, customary, accepted social necessity, and further creating the feeling that the nondrinker is a stupid back number. One of the highest paid advertising lobbyists in the world is placed in Hollywood by the liquor interests. It is his business to see that liquor is used in every possible picture and that nothing is said or done in any movie which will indicate drinking has undesirable effects. Some of the best brains in the advertising industry have become rich subtly exploiting the susceptibility of the average person to the suggestion that drinking booze is a mark of hospitality, breeding, distinction, and culture. Moreover advertising money has often effectively gagged editorial criticism of liquor and deleted mention of alcohol as the cause of accidents in news stories.

It's high time men of real distinction refused to be the victims of this kind of offensive, lying, deadly propaganda. It's time some people of true distinction took the leadership in cracking that vicious social pressure. They would find many friends on their side. To have the moral courage of one's convictions not to drink when others do—that is the true mark of distinction! Anyone can conform. The truly free and independent person is not the one who boasts he is free to drink. Of course he is free to drink. But he's only a slave to convention half the time. The really free person is the one who is free not to drink. I would hate to have to admit that I was so bankrupt of character, mind, and personality that my popularity, well-being, social acceptability, or my career was dependent on consuming alcohol against my better judgment or principles.

The so-called men of distinction—movie stars and socialites who get paid fabulous sums for the use of their pictures in the liquor ads—don't dare tell the whole story.

What about the story of an intoxicated man who wrecked a wagon of hayriders, many of whom were severely injured, one night driving his car home from a party? Not surely a man of distinction? Yes, socially prominent and tops in his profession.

What about the story of a dead man whose body lay unclaimed in a morgue for days? Dead from alcohol! Not a man of distinction? Sure! Just a few years before he was a famous personality with an international reputation as a musician—his name in lights and a household word, with an income of $6,000 a week.

What about the story of a man found dead in his hotel room, his body, head, and walls spattered with his own blood as he literally dashed himself to death against the walls of his room in a drunken frenzy? A man of distinction? Sure! At one time a popular big league ball player.

What about the story of a mother found so drunk in her home that her neglected baby had to be taken from her for proper care and she had to be sent to the hospital? On Skid Row? No, in a mansion in a fashionable residential area.

There are other stories, thousands of them, of people of education and culture who have found the other end of the liquor lure to be a ghastly experience of wrecked homes, diseased and degraded lives, lost jobs, bitter defeat; stories of high-school students on drunken sprees, stories of the college men who hit Skid Row.

It's time for those who have no taste for the whole business to resist this social pressure and to set their own pattern. Let "No, thanks. I don't drink" become a password among those who are adult and wise enough to know it's smarter not to drink.

Young people, business leaders, and hostesses who have had the courage to stand by their convictions on this point discover that they have the respect rather than the ridicule of those people whose opinion counts for anything. The head of a national business said that they had become so disgusted with excessive drinking at their national convention they had cut it out at all dinners and meetings. The response had been wonderful. The way is open for hostesses and executives to deglamorize and depopularize drinking. If those who have convictions on the subject would lead the way, it could be done.

III

Men of real distinction are responsible enough to know that they cannot escape the implications and penalties of their own acts, and are willing to *exercise self-restraint for public welfare*. There are many sincere Christian people who would agree that widespread drinking is to be condemned and yet insist that they find no harm and much innocent pleasure in a quiet cocktail in the home or club or with friends. Moreover they feel they want their children to learn to hold their liquor like gentlemen. It would be nice if the matter were as simple as that, but the very nature of alcohol itself won't let the matter stop there. There are several considerations which deserve a hearing with such people.

Consider the powerful factor of example upon children. Cocktails were so customary in one fine-looking home that even the preacher was offered them! The son of the home, a recent college graduate, was at that very time in a hospital—the victim of a nervous breakdown induced by alcoholism. Yet the parents apparently were oblivious to any connection between their innocent cocktail drinking in the home and their boy's terrible plight.

A Gallup survey showed that the greatest percentage of drinkers is in the 21-29 age group. And the Yale School of Alcoholic Studies reports that two thirds of all alcoholics began their drinking in early high-school days, encouraged by the example of drinking in their homes. Youth drinking needs to be laid at the door of adults. Many a young person, influenced to drink quite innocently by the example of adults, has found himself in the grip of a consuming habit. A real man of distinction would want no part of a custom that contributes so largely to the moral degeneracy of youth—in the family or in the nation. Men of distinction should be men of conscience and responsibility.

All drinking gives indirect support to the underworld. The sordid, crooked, vicious alliance of liquor with rotten politics, corruption of the courts, prostitution, gambling, racketeering, vice, and moral degeneracy in all their brutal and ugly forms is an alliance thinking people would not want to countenance or support either directly or indirectly, in any way, shape, or form. Unfortunately the private drinker cannot be isolated from the public evils of the liquor traffic. Much of our crime and vice is spawned in taverns. Much of the underworld is protected by liquor money at the top. The liquor industry directly or indirectly helps to countenance, defend, and support the dirty work of the social vultures—gamblers, hoodlums, racketeers, degenerates, and gangsters. Of no other legitimate industry can this be said.

Consider the effect of apparently innocent average drinking. Robert V. Seliger of Johns Hopkins has said:

Too many business executives and professional men are to be found in this social drinking bracket. It is my personal conviction, based on experience and psychiatry, that our social drinkers actually cause more trouble of more kinds as a group than do all true alcoholics. Bourbonized judgment causes a loss of millions to investing stockholders. . . . That little drink, medically, is a narcotic drug substance and can be compared with a shot of morphine.

The person who needs a little drink to help him feel good is emotionally upset. He needs a dose of spiritual medicine, not liquor. The life that has to be drugged to escape boredom is built on rotten foundations.

Alcohol is a habit-forming intoxicant that dulls the nervous system, retards muscular reaction, and destroys the inhibitions that make man better than the beast. Used so often under the excuse that it is a stimulant, it proves in reality to be an anesthetic. It numbs the feelings of the body and blocks the higher brain cells. It has this effect in any amount and in any form. As such it is an implacable enemy of human life and personality. Moreover the late Charles Mayo of the Mayo Clinic stated that 3 out of every 10 who use alcohol in moderation become heavy drinkers. No one can tell until it is too late whether he will be one of them. It is not alcoholism but the nature of alcohol itself that is at the root of all the trouble. The emphasis on alcoholism that has received so much attention lately is really a smoke screen that obscures the real seat of the trouble. The liquor industry itself is against alcoholism. However, only a small part of all the damaging influence of drinking comes from the alcoholics. To be sure they are sick and need treatment. But what of the inherent narcotic, poisonous effect of alcohol on the lives and homes of those who never become alcoholic? What of the stupidity of waiting until people become alcoholic before dealing with the cause of the trouble? In no other therapy, personal or social, is the treatment confined to the effect, alcoholism, and not the cause, alcohol.

Consider too the kind of age we live in. It is an electronic, superscientific, highly mechanized world. It is a time when all moral values are in jeopardy. The world, literally seems to tremble on the edge of doom. We need now, if ever in history, nerves, minds, hands, and character that are as steady and clear as humanly possible if we are to cope with the titantic problems clamoring at our door. In an atomic age instead of being glorified drinking should be anathema if men are to survive. It should not take a man of distinction to see that.

What is the conclusion to all this? Admittedly it is a knotty problem not easily solved. Does the solution lie in a program of education or in the banning of liquor advertising in interstate commerce? Is the extension of local option desirable? Should some form of state licensed and operated bottled liquor dispensaries be advocated? These programs are not the issue now. Prior to any attempt at public control must come an aroused public conscience on the subject. And this aroused conscience should be under the leadership of the Christian Church and the Christian ministry. How long are Christian leaders going to be intimidated by the false and vicious propaganda of the liquor traffic which undercuts and nullifies the program of the Church in our society? We are greatly concerned about problems of poverty, housing, slums, crime, racial prejudice. We have not, however, been willing to recognize that liquor is the basis of much of the social degradation we deplore in these areas. We must recover from our sense of helplessness. These problems can be solved because they must be solved.

What we need are more men of real distinction. When the freedom to do as we please involves the approval and support of a custom that has so many damaging effects on life and society, then men of *real* distinction are properly the kind of men who are big enough to recognize their leadership responsibility.

The man of real distinction first of all lends the influence of his example by refusing to drink. The man of real distinction encourages his friends and associates to do the same. The man of real distinction supports organizations that seek to educate for truth in this field. The man of real distinction knows that the words of Abraham Lincoln are true: "Whether or not the world would be vastly benefited by a total and final banishment from it of all intoxicating drinks seems to me not now an open question. Three fourths of mankind confess the affirmative with their tongues, and, I believe, all the rest acknowledge it in their hearts."

144

THANKSGIVING DAY

The Spirit of Thanksgiving

Enter into his gates with thanksgiving.
—Ps. 100:4

FULTON OURSLER IN ONE OF HIS BOOKS TELLS OF HIS OLD Negro nurse, Anna Maria Cecily Sophia Virginia Avalon Thessalonians, who was born a slave on the eastern shore of Maryland and who had attended the birth of his mother and his own birth. She taught him his greatest lesson of the thankful heart.

I remember her as she sat at the kitchen table in our house; the hard old brown hands folded across her starched wrapper, the glistening black eyes lifted to the whitewashed ceiling, and the husky old whispering voice saying, "Much obliged, Lord, for my vittles." "Anna," I asked, "what's a vittle?" . . . "It's what I've got to eat and drink, that's vittles." . . . "But you'd get your vittles whether you thanked the Lord or not." . . . "Sure, but it makes everything taste better to be thankful."

After the meal she thanked the Lord again and then said: "You know, it's a funny thing about being thankful—it's a game an old colored preacher taught me to play. It's looking for things to be thankful for. You don't know how many of them you pass right by unless you go looking for them. . . . Take this morning. I wake up and lay there lazy-like wondering what I got to be thankful for now. And you know what, I can't think of anything to thank him for. . . . And then from the kitchen comes the most

145

delicious morning smell that ever tickled my old nose. Coffee. Much obliged, Lord, for the coffee, . . . much obliged for the smell of it!" [1]

There came a time when Oursler went through a very trying and bitter period of discouragement and failure. He said the memory of Anna's spirit of thanksgiving gave him a handle to work with, and it literally pulled him up and out and onward. Then he was called to the bedside of the dying Anna, old, crippled, feeble. Standing beside her and noting her hands knitted together in pain, he wondered what she would have to be thankful for now.

She opened her eyes, smiled, and the last words she spoke were: "Much obliged, Lord, for such fine friends."

How often a weary and lonely way may be lighted by the glory of the thankful heart. Among the simple blessings of life we take selfishly for granted we need to say, "Much obliged for the vittles, Lord."

Because of the turmoil of our world this thankful spirit needs wider and deeper expression.

I

It needs to express itself in *national gratitude unspoiled by private greed*. We are guilty of the grossest sin to enjoy the benefits of a land of peace, plenty, security, and freedom without a profound sense of humble gratitude to almighty God. We are a nation of fussers and complainers. The fact is, however, this nation now is more favored as a people than any other nation at any time in history.

[1] From *The Precious Secret*, published by the John C. Winston Company. Used by permission.

We have 1,000,000,000 acres of farm land; 500,000,000 acres of forest; 100,000,000 acres of coal, iron, copper, and other mineral lands; 34,000,000 acres of rivers and lakes; 100,000,000 acres of developed city land; and 316,000 oil wells. We have 6,500,000 farms; 185,000,000 horses, mules, cows, sheep, and swine; 500,000,000 chickens, turkeys, and ducks; 37,000,000 buildings, factories, schools, libraries, and homes; 127,000,000 major machines, such as turbines, locomotives, and looms; 2,000,000 miles of surfaced highways; 250,000 miles of railroads; 59,000 miles of navigable waterways; 737,000 miles of pipeline; 160,000 miles of electric power transmission lines.

For the benefit of those who say the American system is a failure we should look at the record. We have 62,000,000 people employed. With only 7 per cent of the world's population we have 80 per cent of the autos, 50 per cent of the telephones, 60 per cent of all the life insurance policies. We have one radio for every three people, compared with one for every ninety in Russia. It is no news that the American industrial worker enjoys more comforts, luxuries, and leisure than his counterpart anywhere else in the world. In 1940, for example, he could earn a moderately priced automobile with 853 hours of labor. In England it took 3,522 hours of work to pay for a similar car; in France, 7,295 hours; in Germany, 5,054 hours.

The words of publisher John S. Knight express the thought well:

For one I grow exceedingly weary of hearing how the capitalistic system is on trial. On trial for what? Has any other system accomplished as much or provided better standards of living? Why isn't socialism on trial in England? Or communism in

Russia and her satellite states? If capitalism is through why are we asked to provide the food, the money, the tools to rebuild Europe?

Our vast national strength and wealth call for genuine gratitude. But our greed can spoil it all. Our own private greed, in which our very freedom and plenty give full opportunity to indulge, is one of our worst enemies.

It is the greed of the producer, on the farm or in the factory, who selfishly reaches for longer profits out of the distress of humanity.

It is the greed of government which maintains itself in power by an army of needless employees supported by ever-increasing taxes.

It is the greed of the distributor who takes advantage of a distress situation to gouge the buyer for unreasonable price markups.

It is the greed of the labor boss who is shortsighted enough to imperil and disregard the law in order to gain ends difficult to justify.

It is the greed of the gaudy rich whose vulgar display of the trappings of wealth is a vicious commentary on democratic culture.

It is the greed of industrial profiteers who side-step competition by joining with others to raise prices beyond the demands of a fair profit.

It is the greed of the extortionist who would sell out the general welfare for his own gain.

Our prosperity will be our undoing if we cannot curb the greed of men. Have American people the capacity to enjoy and be grateful for their prosperity and not let it be spoiled by the greed of the heart? That is the question.

We say we do not want more governmental controls. But it still remains to be proved that we have the moral and spiritual power to control by our own accord the tremendous resources that are ours. Only as we strengthen and develop our spiritual powers and disciplines can we keep the very magnitude of the wealth that is ours from destroying us. Only thus can we use it for the welfare and freedom of mankind.

II

The thankful spirit expresses itself in *compassion without softness*. We hear reports of distress and tragic conditions around the world. We hear of children taking turns to go to unheated schools so that they can wear enough clothes, their brothers and sisters meanwhile staying in bed. We hear of families living like animals crowded in cellars and wrecked rooms of bombed buildings. We hear of thirty million who must die of starvation in Europe until the Continent can feed itself. We hear of bundles by the roadside in China and India—the bodies of those who have died from starvation.

The hearts of all decent Americans are deeply moved and stirred by the wretched plight of our brother men in the wastelands of the world. The United States seeks to use its tremendous resources to help the stricken needy. It would be nice if we did not have to qualify that statement. But we shall have to be wise, or our generosity will prove our gullibility. In our desire to be helpful both in relief and reconstruction we must beware that we do not play into the hands of those who would destroy us along with Europe and Asia.

We are told that the character and generosity of America are being offset in every possible way by the false and vicious propaganda of the communists. Well, let us be generous to a fault. In our desire to help, however, let us not be dupes to the point of hurting rather than helping those who are the objects of our concern. We do this when we give support to a program which holds us up to contempt and ridicule. Why help those who will not help themselves? Why help those who would destroy us? Let us be softhearted, yes, but not softheaded to the point of wrecking our own democracy. If we are to save the people of western Europe for democracy, let us do it in the name and under the banner of democracy and Christianity—unashamed, unabashed, unafraid, and unintimidated by lies.

This is no place to debate the Marshall Plan. It is the place, however, to say that aid to Europe should be safeguarded in every possible way. It must not provide arms which in turn will be used against us. It must not be dissipated by the hands of racketeers, profiteers, black marketeers, or made a political or military football by demagogues. These would use American goods and gold to further selfish causes and private ambitions. That can happen here and abroad. When it does, democracy loses and communism gains.

As America shares in the reconstruction in Europe, let it be under direct supervision of American engineers, industrialists, and Christian relief workers. Here is a chance to show that the American system works and the American spirit is equal to the hour of the world's great need.

III

This thanksgiving spirit expresses itself in *freedom undiluted by careless forgetfulness.* In Rushville's East Hill Cemetery at the foot of a fifteen-foot granite cross there is an open book sculptured by Malvina Hoffman, marking the grave of a man who believed devoutly in America. On the open face of the book are engraved some of Wendell Willkie's own words:

I believe in America because in it we are free. Free to choose our government, to speak our minds, to observe different religions. . . . Because we are generous with our freedom and share our rights with those who disagree with us. . . . Because we hate no people and covet no people's land. . . . Freedom is an indivisible word. We must have faith that the welfare of one is the welfare of all. . . . Only the productive are strong. . . . Only the strong are free.

Thanksgiving time is a good time to celebrate the kind of freedom that our forefathers sought. But too often the cry for freedom is a cry for license. Free enterprise, yes— so long as it gives the strong a chance to exploit the weak. Free religion, surely—but then never darken the doors of the church. Free schools, certainly—then pay teachers a below-subsistence salary. Free press, to be sure—then boycott papers that offer different opinions. Free speech, by all means—then refuse a hearing to the other side. Free politics, yes—then outlaw anyone who votes a different party slate.

Freedom is our greatest blessing. It is hard to win and easy to lose. Where did freedom come from? We must never forget that it is ours solely because of men who believed in God first. It is lost as men lose that faith. Our

Pilgrim Fathers may have had their faults, but the freedom they believed in came from their faith in God.

It has been pointed out:

The same revolutionary spirit produced vastly different results in France and America. In France liberty became license, the age of reason brought on the Reign of Terror, and the end was a Dictator, Napoleon, who left all Europe staggering in ruins for thirty years. The same revolutionary spirit in America resulted in a Constitution, a democratic form of government, and a George Washington, as the leader of our national destiny. Why this difference? It was because of the Pilgrims and Puritans of New England, the Quakers of Pennsylvania, and the Catholics of Maryland. America was founded upon a rock, because God was given a place in the minds of the people.[2]

We dare not forget that only as faith in God lives are men free. That makes the program of the Church of God the most significant and far-reaching enterprise on earth today.

[2] From the July, 1943, issue of *The Pulpit*. Used by permission.

UNIVERSAL BIBLE SUNDAY

On Rediscovering the Bible

The entrance of thy words giveth light.
—Ps. 119:130

AN EIGHTEENTH-CENTURY SKEPTIC IS SAID TO HAVE DE-clared: "It took twelve men to establish Christianity. I will show the world that one man can pull it to pieces. In one hundred years the Bible will become an obsolete book, to be relegated to the dusty shelves of the antiquarian."

The time is more than up. In spite of the scoffers that have come and gone the Bible is far from being obsolete. Indeed, it is in greater demand than at any other time in history. It has been estimated that our printing presses turn out an average of one Bible every 6 seconds, day and night, the year around. That means 10 Bibles every minute, 600 copies every hour, 14,400 copies every day in the year. On a single day a few years ago there were printed 9 tons of Bibles in 28 different languages!

Dr. Frank Luther Mott in his book *Golden Multitudes,* a story of best sellers, lists twenty-one books that have sold more than two million copies each. These include *Alice in Wonderland, Ben-Hur, Little Women, Robinson Crusoe, Tom Sawyer,* and Shakespeare's plays, along with *How to Win Friends and Influence People.* It is interesting to note that five of the twenty-one named are based directly on the Bible, including *In His Steps*, *The Robe*, and Hurlburt's *Story of the Bible*. About half the total sales of all twenty-one may be accounted for by one of this biblical group, *In His Steps*. The combined copies of all these twenty-one top best sellers amounted to about sixty-five million. On the other hand the Bible itself has sold about two billion copies.

This enormous production of the Bible does not of itself guarantee that the truth of the Scriptures becomes the light of men. It does indicate, however, that men in need through the centuries have felt that here was salvation. Even in our tangled times we can again discover in its message the way out and up.

I

We need to rediscover the importance of the Bible *in the life of the nation*. In the rotunda of the Capitol building in Washington there is a great painting, "Embarkation of the Pilgrims," painted by the American artist Robert Walter Weir under commission from the Congress of the United States. We should be forever grateful to that artist that in the focal point of the picture, the center of the group gathered on the deck of the "Speedwell," is the open Bible, held in the hands of William Brewster. In a time when American democracy is held in contempt we need to have burned upon our national conscience the full meaning of that picture. It means that America, her freedoms, and her finest ideals were founded upon the open Bible. These will be preserved only as the messages of that Book live among us.

"Did we bring the Bible to these shores?" asks Odel Shepard. "Did it not rather bring us? The breath of ancient prophets was in the sails that drove the tiny 'Mayflower.' The hope and faith of ancient prophets, poets, kings, and lawyers were in the hearts of those who first sang the Lord's song in this strange land."

Let us make no mistake. Although it is the Constitution that guarantees freedom of worship, it is the Church that guarantees the freedom of the open Bible. Those who look with indifference upon the Church need to heed the words of Alexis de Tocqueville, the great French student of American democracy. In accounting for the growing power of America he reported to his own people:

> Sirs, I went at your bidding; I ascended their mountains; I went down into their valleys; I visited their commercial markets and their emporiums of trade; I entered their legislative halls and their judicial courts. I searched everywhere in vain until I entered the church. It was there, sirs, as I listened to the soul-elevating and soul-equalizing gospel as it fell from Sabbath to Sabbath upon the waiting multitudes, that I learned why America is great and free and France is slave.

Wherever the Church becomes the state church, men are held in slavery. In the face of the Roman Catholic Church's bid for political power in America we need to recall that the struggle of men to secure and hold God-given rights to translate, read, and interpret the Scriptures for themselves has been a long, fierce, and bloody conflict. If we think the struggle is over, we are wrong. Here is a statement of the Roman Catholic Church about the Bible: "It should be perfectly clear to anyone that the Bible is not a safe guide in matters of religion, because it is not now and never has been accessible to all people, because it is not perfectly clear and intelligible to all: and because it does not contain all religious truth." The liberties we Americans hold dear as life itself are at stake, therefore, in our treatment of this open Book. As Thomas Marshall put it, "If I were to have my way, I would take the torch out of the hand of the Statue of Liberty in New York Harbor and in its place put the open Bible."

II

We need to rediscover the Bible *in the education of youth*.

Dr. Roy Ross, who for many years has been one of the foremost leaders in religious education, loves to tell the story of a group of children gathered at a home one time. The mother asked each to give a Bible verse. Several of the children did so. Little Johnny said he did not know any.

"Don't you go to Sunday school?" said the mother.

"Why, no," the little boy answered. "We have religious education at our church."

To be sure, memorizing the Bible verses alone does not lead to a discovery of the meaning of the Bible in human lives. Moreover, newer methods of religious education have real value. Yet the studied neglect of the Bible in the education of children is failing to give our youth a foundation for character that comes in no other way. Likewise it overlooks an appreciation of one of the great sources not only of truth, but of art, of literature, and many other phases of our culture. This is much the same as banning, burning, or discrediting the one most important Book of all. Let a child learn by heart some of the great passages of Scripture and be familiar with the great stories of the Bible, and he will have something to hold on to all through life.

156

In certain high-school English classes the teachers conducted a survey of Bible knowledge. They discovered that 88 per cent of the students did not know even what the four Gospels were. One student guessed they were: "love, honor, cherish, and obey." Another said that three of them were "Christianity, Hinduism, and Confusion." It seemed that 98 per cent had never heard of Saul of Tarsus. Incidentally every single student asked that he be told the answers.

A few years ago Headmaster Leslie Sveringhaus at Harvard School for Boys tested 252 boys aged thirteen to eighteen on quotations from song hits and from the Bible. They were asked to finish the lines from songs such as the following: "All or nothing at all, half . . ."; "Long ago and far away, I . . ."; "We meet and the . . ."; "Don't sit under . . ."; "If your heart goes bumpity bump . . ."

They were also asked to complete Bible verses like these: "Honour thy father and thy mother: that . . ."; "Why beholdest thou the mote that . . ."; "For what shall it profit a man, if . . ."; "Thou preparest a table before me in . . ."; "Suffer the little children . . ."; "Now abideth faith, hope, and charity, these three: but . . ."

The headmaster exacted word-for-word accuracy on the song titles but accepted approximations on the Bible verses. Results: The school average on the songs was 56 per cent, on the Bible 23 per cent. There were 45 boys who got all the Bible lines wrong; 157 got 50 per cent or less. And these were privileged boys from the best homes, the future leaders of the nation! The problem is not confined to high school. A University of Missouri professor of English mentioned one time, "Am I my brother's keeper?" Not one in a class of thirty-three had any idea as to the source of the quotation.

Not all high-school and college students should be Bible scholars. But something is deficient in our total educational program in a professedly Christian land founded on the Bible when our children grow to maturity in complete ignorance of this greatest single civilizing, cultural, and literary source and force in history and in life. There is no danger to freedom of religion in having some kind of Bible study included in the schools of the country. This can be done wisely and well. When Frank Sparks, a Christian businessman, was president of Wabash College, he made religion a required course for freshmen. Immediately there was a howl from the faculty. "Religion is a part of our civilization," Sparks replied. "We force no doctrine down our students' throats. We merely introduce them to the history of religions, the history of the Bible, and the application of Christian principles to our economic, social, and political problems. I doubt that this study will harm any young man."

Our own church schools are partly to blame. There are about sixteen million children in America who are today unreached by Sunday schools. Take Washington, D.C., as an example. In four years there was a population increase of 36 per cent, a church membership increase of 11 per cent, and a Sunday-school decrease of 10 per cent.

No wonder, then, church-school enrollment needs to be emphasized so that the Bible and its message may be made a part of the instruction and grounding of youth as a preparation for life. God's moral and spiritual truths are as important as arithmetic and geography. The basic foundation of Christian living that springs from a vital acquaintance with the Bible is far more important for modern youth in our kind of world than a knowledge of Latin or chemistry.

III

We need to rediscover a truer, more satisfying conception and use of the Bible *in our own personal living*. One big reason why the Bible has been of such little help to many people is that it has been misused, mistreated, and misinterpreted. We treat the Bible in a mechanical, literalistic, superstitious manner. We use it somewhat as our forebears used certain supposedly infallible cures endorsed in the almanacs of colonial times. Eleanor Merriam lists some of these: Rubbing onions and honey on the head to cure baldness; stuffing orange rinds up the nostrils to cure a cold; dropping juice of rotten apples in the eyes to cure dull sight; cleaning the teeth with ashes of burned bread; and curing toothache by rubbing the feet with warm bran water.

Many people even in our day treat the Bible in a similar primitive vein. It is used too often as a charm to bring luck or as a smoke screen to chase away the evil spirits. James Claypool of the American Bible Society tells of a chaplain who was approached by a soldier who asked seriously for the verse in the Bible that would stop bleeding. He said that if you put one hand on a certain verse and the other hand on an injury, the bleeding would stop. In Greybull, Wyoming, a girl four years old died of spinal meningitis because her parents refused to take her to a doctor or to allow the county health officer to examine her. Why? Her parents, members of no church, declared they "were looking to the Lord to cure Frances June because they believed in the

Lord's promises in the Bible." It is the same hocus-pocus attitude toward Scripture that is behind the people who handle snakes as an expression of religious faith in keeping with Luke 10:19, "Behold, I give unto you power to tread on serpents . . . : and nothing shall by any means hurt you." Likewise oversimplified and unbelievable literalism leads many otherwise sensible people into many a fantastic and weird cult. These find a proof text in the Bible for almost any kind of religious malformation. They do a disservice to the plain man's understanding of the Word.

The Bible, however, does not deal in magic. It deals in truth: the really fundamental truths of the fatherhood of God, the worth and brotherhood of man, the salvation of the soul from sin, the divine redemption of the race, the possibility of the Kingdom of God. Every confusing, difficult, and isolated passage needs to be interpreted in the light of this wider mission and purpose of the total Scriptures.

We need to know the Bible for what it is and not try to make of it something it is not. It is a record of man's search for God and of God's search for man. Against the paganism, cynicism, and defeatism of our day it is a source book for the soul, with its perennial gifts of courage, hope, faith, and comfort. Here is the great arsenal of the spirit wherein men forge divine weapons for the struggle of existence. Here are bread of life, meat and drink for the inner man, light for many a darkened way. Here, of all the great books, is the one great Book.

Those who persist in grubbing about only in Revelation or Genesis or Ecclesiastes don't know the Bible. We must not lose the Bible's meaning for us because of the exaggeration of some overzealous champions. If we do, we miss the power for living as expressed by the thundering prophet, "Let justice run down as waters, and righteousness as a mighty stream"; the inspiration of the song of the psalmist, "Thou madest him a little lower than the angels; thou crownest him with glory and honour"; the beauty and appeal of the Master, "Come unto me all ye that labour and are heavy laden, and I will give you rest"; the challenge of Paul, "Forgetting those things which are behind . . . , I press toward the mark for the prize of the high calling of God in Christ Jesus." Here is the core of the Bible. We don't need to be scholars to discover it calling to the highest in us, giving us the long view and the counsel of patience, always with the shining promise that a better world is possible.

CHRISTMAS

On Putting Christ into Christmas

Behold, I bring you good tidings of great joy.
—Luke 2:10

ON JULY 14, 1789, JEAN LENOIR, A COBBLER LIVING IN AN obscure side street in Paris, wrote in his diary: "Nothing of importance happened today." Just a short distance away was the Bastille, and on that very day a mob had stormed it. They killed the troops, freed the prisoners, destroyed the building, and started the French Revolution. This event changed the whole course of the life of France.

So, too often, it is with us at Christmas time. Busy with routine details of the holiday season, we are apt to ignore the fact that Christmas marks the birthday of Jesus, the most revolutionary event in history. Long accustomed to the chores of Christmas, we oftentimes go through the motions of celebration without being aware that Christmas can have any real meaning for our own hearts.

Consider then the importance of putting Christ into our Christmas. For it is important that we ourselves gather with the Wise Men and shepherds before the manger of Bethlehem that cradles the King. There is nothing quite so gaudily and noisily out of place as Christmas without Christ.

I

When we put Christ into Christmas, *our hearts are revived by a renewed sense of the divine at the heart of life.* On February 24, 1948, one of the most unusual operations in medical history took place in Ohio State University's department of research surgery. A stony sheath was removed from around the heart of Harry Beshara, a man thirty years of age. When only a boy he had been shot accidentally by a playmate with a .22-caliber rifle. The bullet had lodged in his heart but had not caused death. However, a lime deposit had begun to form over the protective covering of the heart and gradually was strangling it. The operation was a delicate one involving the separation of the ribs and moving the left lung to one side. Then the stony coating was lifted from the heart as an orange is peeled. Immediately the pressure on the heart was reduced, and it responded by expanding and pumping normally. "I feel a thousand per cent better already," said the patient soon after the operation.

There is a parable of life here. Our hearts develop a hard protective coating because of accidents and incidents of life. They are coated by the deposits of a thousand deceits and rebuffs. They are hardened by the pressures of circumstance. Inevitably they become smothered and insensitive to the divine. Ever so gradually we find it easier to sneer than to pray. It becomes simpler to work than to worship. Self-satisfied, proud, often cynical, our hearts need a spiritual operation that only Christmas can perform when we dare to surrender our hearts' burden before the cradle of Bethlehem.

In the shadow of that little town on the wondrous night of long ago a ragged little boy watched the procession of the kings and noblemen with their chests of rare gifts for the Christ Child. His eyes filled with tears. "If only a pearl would fall from the hand of a king, then I could go too. But I am ashamed to go. I have no gift for the Saviour."

He was about to turn and run into the hills. Suddenly an angel appeared before him out of the night and said, "Give what is closest to your heart." They say that a bright star, the Christmas star, appeared in the heavens over Bethlehem as a ragged boy placed a faded blue sack beside the rubies, the gold pieces, the myrrh and frankincense. It contained the things closest to his heart: a sea shell that whispered in his ears, a piece of rope used to climb high trees, a jagged slingshot made from a forked limb, and a butterfly preserved in candlewax.

"The tapering years have moulded many things since that night in Bethlehem." During those years men have discovered a wondrous thing. When in quiet adoration they bring to the Master the things dearest to them, the tough coating of their hearts is lifted, and stars appear in their skies again.

Phillips Osgood puts this idea in these words:

He who devotes his utmost to the immediate is the creature of the temporary and insignificant. Exclusively to identify my life with the materialistic will be to make myself the slave of the accidental. If the mundane thing to which I have harnessed myself goes to flinders, I myself go with it; I have no stance for the abiding. . . . I stand or fall with the accidental—money, power, fame—if the accidental is my goal. But if I am caught up by the glories which shine in the highest realities; if I bind myself, no matter in what awesome humility, to the values which motivate

164

the universe; if I take for my ideal such a life as that of the Christ who lives in God, the spirit behind all values, worths, beauties, and joys; if I, too, lift up my life to God, I shall be above the swirl of the accidental; I shall have the infinite coursing through me.[1]

We are like the man in the fable who had a mania for building towers. He finally succeeded in building one tower with eleven thousand stairs. Nothing like it had been made before. He was very proud. He was about to congratulate himself on his accomplishment. Then standing on top of his tower, he looked up and saw the stars above!

God grant us the grace at Christmas to pause in our stair building—our labor and our concerns—and look up and see stars. At least see the one star leading to the Christ of Christmas. Our hearts are revived by a renewed sense of the divine at the heart of life.

II

When we put Christ into Christmas, *our spirits are lightened by the reawakening of our sense of joy.* One of the most dramatic scenes in European history occurred when Charles VIII demanded ransom from the free city of Florence. Capponi, the mayor, refused to give a groat. Charles thundered threats. "I will have my trumpets blown," he blustered.

Capponi's answer is immortal. "Blow your trumpets," he shouted. "Blow your trumpets, and we will ring our bells!"

Charles was silent after this, for at the ringing of the bells the hidden army of Florence would spring into being.

This story suggests the resources of the Christian in the

[1] From *The Pulpit*. Used by permission.

face of the blustering threats of life. "Behold, I bring you good tidings of great joy, . . . for unto you is born this day in the city of David a Saviour, which is Christ the Lord." Thank God that ever since that heavenly announcement the Christian has had the bells of joy ringing their music of faith and hope in his heart.

There is so much to weight us down, to burden our souls, to depress our minds, to undermine our spirits—so many doubts, so many heartaches, so many regrets, so many disappointments, so many mysteries, so many fears. In our moments of weakness their trumpets of defeat blow many a mournful blast. How shall we answer them save by the bells of joy that become real in our hearts when we put Christ into Christmas?

Almost every Christmas hymn has the dominant note of joy:

> Dear Desire of every nation,
>   Joy of every longing heart.

> Rejoice! Rejoice! Immanuel.

> Joyful, all ye nations, rise,
>   Join the triumph of the skies.

> Love, joy, and hope, like flowers,
>   Spring in his path to birth.

> Glad tidings of great joy I bring,
>   To you and all mankind.

> Joy to the world! the Saviour reigns:
>   Let men their songs employ.

As with gladness men of old
Did the guiding star behold;
As with joy they hailed its light,

Leading onward, beaming bright.
　　Till the air,
　　Everywhere,
　　Now with joy is ringing.

With them the joyful tidings first begun
Of God Incarnate and the Virgin's Son.

Sing, choirs of angels, sing in exultation.

　　We rejoice in the light,
　　And we echo the song.

To you the joyous news we bring.

　　Good Christian men, rejoice,
　　With heart and soul and voice;
　　Give ye heed to what we say:
　　Jesus Christ is born today.

Who said that the Christian faith is a long-faced, grim, gloomy affair of negative restrictions and sad-eyed resignation? There's nothing dreary about the faith of the Christian when Christ is at the center of Christmas! The Christian's very birthright is joy and gladness, which are born at Christmas into the original blood stream of the Christian life. This is no surface happiness. It is the inner radiance and lightness of spirit enjoyed by those who live in the presence of the God of triumph and love, revealed in Jesus Christ.

Modern Christians need to recover this sense of joy. We have no right to be downcast and desolate. We ought to be ashamed of ourselves for being so grouchy and pessimistic. We must quit feeding on our doubts and miseries, and begin to cultivate the singing soul and the glowing heart. Our God is a living God, and in him is reason for buoyancy and cause for rejoicing. Joy is revived by a sense of the divine. Christmas is spotlighted by the renewal of joy.

III

When we put Christ into Christmas, *our lives are redeemed by our faith in love* as the greatest thing in the world. High on a hill in Melbourne, Australia, stands a beautiful building known as the Shrine of Remembrance. It commemorates the people's sacrifice during World War I. It is a thing of beauty and majesty with its Doric columns, its pyramidal dome, and its landscaped terraces. The central hall is a great empty room lined with marble pillars. The only object in the room is the Stone of Remembrance, a sheer sheet of marble into which are cut simple words which speak beautifully of the power of love. Overhead in the dome is a small opening. After long and difficult study of the order in the universe, the architect so fixed the position of that opening that at exactly 11:00 o'clock in the morning on November 11 for one thousand years a beam of sunshine will pour down upon the Stone of Remembrance and illumine the one word "Love" in the inscription reading "Greater Love Hath No Man."

This is a very noble gesture of man to show his regard for love as one of the great forces of life. Yet at its best it is a cold and cheerless effort compared with the ever-living monument arranged by the Heavenly Father to remind men through the centuries of the love that saves, lifts, and redeems life. For in the fullness of time the divine Architect of the universe caused the light of divine love to shine upon a child in a stable. Henceforth through all the centuries of time men shall stand in humility and awe at the remembrance of this event. It was an event that enthroned love as the divine law of life.

> Love came down at Christmas,
>   Love all lovely, Love Divine;
> Love was born at Christmas,
>   Star and angels gave the sign.
>
> Worship we the Godhead,
>   Love incarnate, Love Divine;
> Worship we our Jesus;
>   But wherewith for sacred sign?
>
> Love shall be our token,
>   Love be yours and Love be mine,
> Love to God and all men,
>   Love for plea and gift and sign.[2]

Can this love redeem us today from our follies, our stupid hatreds, our sins? Can it cope with the evil forces in our kind of world? Why not dispense with Christ and all this talk of love? The answer is easy: love is our only hope.

A top research chemist of Princeton, Hugh Scott Taylor, made a startling statement not long ago. He said that if we lumped all the sources of power available to men in 1939—steam, electricity, internal combustion engines, TNT, and so on—and called them one, then the potential power available to men just eight years later, in 1947, was forty mil-

[2] Christina Rossetti, "Incarnate Love."

lion times that amount. Is there any counterbalancing power on earth equal to the job of controlling and directing that physical power for the weal instead of the woe of man? Yes, only one. Is it in the military, in the laboratory, in money? No. It is in the power of love. Here is God's everlasting gift to men. No other gift do the weary-footed, fearstricken children of men need more than this. It is a gift free to all for the asking. It is ours when we put Christ at the heart of Christmas.

This love is no weak and spineless thing. It does not spend itself in vague and quieting commonplaces. Nor does it exhaust itself in tarnished tinsel and phony Santa Clauses. It is gentle, kindly, forgiving, and comforting, to be sure. But it is also strong, vital, revolutionary. It is a love that disturbs our easygoing ways with a vision of God's hopes and dreams. It is a love that flames in indignation against greed, crime, war, vice. It is steadfastly opposed to all the ugly and vicious aspects of life which deny God's love and hold in contempt the Christ of Christmas. It is a love that laughs. It is also a love that weeps in agony over the cruel inhumanities and the brutal exploitations of life. It is a love that disturbs our narrow ideas with the awareness that God's gift is for all men. It is a love that gives and suffers in defense of its own against all who hold it in mockery and scorn.

When we put Christ into Christmas, this divine love is born again in our own hearts and homes and world. Without him life becomes stagnant and diseased, bitter and self-destructive. God at Christmas would remind us that love is still supreme. He would have us know that only in its light and power does life have a chance to be cleansed and purified, redeemed and restored.

Christ of all the Christmases there have been, hear my
  prayer for those who have no Christmas.
For the darkened millions who go to bed hungry
  tonight, and all the nights.
For the children in whose homes the candles have been
  put out these days by war, and pestilence and fear.
For boys and girls whose hands press against store windows
  while their eyes devour the glories they can never touch.
For those whose hearts are torn by hate, twisted by prejudice,
  crippled by narrowness and pride.
For these who have no Christmas this day, Christ of deathless
  love, let thy presence come with joy and healing in its wings.[3]

[3] Percy R. Hayward, "For Those Who Have No Christmas," *Young People's Prayers,* published by Association Press. Used by permission.